PHANTOM II

A Pictorial History of the McDonnell Douglas Phantom II

by Lou Drendel

squadron/signal publications

ISBN 0-89747-062-1

Photo Credits

US Navy
USAF
ASMC
McDonnell Douglas
Paul Stevens
Michel Klaver
Jim Sullivan
Charles Howes
Scott Brown
Gunter Grondstein
Norman E. Taylor
Ken Buchanan
Dr. J.G. Handelman
Jerry Geer

If you have photographs of the aircraft, armor, soldiers or ships of any nation, particularly wartime snapshots, why not share them with us and help make Squadron/Signal's books all the more interesting and complete in the future. Any photograph sent to us will be copied and the original returned. The donor will be fully credited for any photos used. Please send them to: Squadron/Signal Publications Inc., 1115 Crowley Dr., Carrollton, TX 75006.

Introduction

I have always been an airplane "nut". My preoccupation with aeronautica dates back to a childhood filled with the feats of the great airmen and aircraft of World War II and Korea. Somehow, in the late fifties and early sixties, I lost my status as an airplane enthusiast. Oh, I still knew a Spitfire from a Sabre, but the late models might just as well not have existed, for all I knew. (or cared) Looking back on it now, I realize that my malaise was not uncommon. Specifically, it was a preoccupation with girls and fast cars. Anyway, I lost the better part of a decade of aeronautical advances because of it. When I finally awoke to find myself married and driving a four door Chevelle, I realized that I had a lot of catching up to do if I was to regain my status of an aerophile.

So, sometime in 1964, I hied myself down to the local bookstore, intent on catching up on the latest models of the Sabre and Thunderjet. The first book I picked up on modern aircraft had a picture of the F-4 Pahntom on the cover. I was thunderstruck! What had happened to sleek jets? This thing had a droopy nose, bent wings, and it looked as though the stabilizer was about to fall off. And it

was big! I checked the photo caption ... yes ... it does say "F", so it must be a fighter. But the more I looked at that picture (and others inside the book), the more the F-4 seemed to shed it's ugliness. It took on character, personality, and it's performance figures shouted SPACEAGE! What great advances had been wrought while I had piddled away my time on mere girls! (I realized suddenly that this singular thought had reinstated me as a full-fledged airplane nut, regardless of my lack of current knowledge of the subject.)

Over the intervening years I have expanded my knowledge of modern military aircraft, but the Phantom, like a first love, retains a special place in my enthusiast's heart. It was the first jet fighter I flew in, and the subject of the first "In Action" title I authored. I'm sure I have built more models of the Phantom, and done more paintings of it than any other airplane I can think of, including the endless succession of P-51's I turned out when I was eight years old. So I am especially happy to be doing another book on it, and I hope that this volume adds to what we did in the first.

A Legend in it's Own Time

It is the most prolific of modern fighters, with the 5,000th example due to be rolled out in 1978. (Assuming the almost certain continuation of production through that year.) It will have acheived the notable milestone of being in continuous production for a full two decades. This, in itself, is amazing if you consider the giant technological strides aerospace has taken over that span of time. The Phantom II has taken them all in stride, proving itself the very epitome of adaptability, embracing not only solid state technology, but new careers and missions with equal aplomb. It remains the first string tactical fighter of the USAF and U.S. Marines. It continues to serve with the U.S. Navy. It serves with the RAF, Royal Navy, Israel, Iran, Greece, Spain, Turkey, South Korea, West Germany, Australia, and Japan. It has acheived a place in the pantheon of fighter aircraft that may never be approached by another design. It is truly a legend ... a worldwide legend ... in it's own time.

Beginnings

The Phantom might well have been dubbed "Phoenix", for it was born out of the ashes of a lost competition for a carrier-based fighter. It was 1953, and Chance Vought had successfully demonstrated their F8U Crusader. It was a bitter pill for McDonnell to swallow, for they had established a reputation for producing what the Navy wanted, starting with the first jet powered carrier fighter, the Phantom I, and continuing through the Banshee and Demon series. In fact, McDonnell did not swallow their loss to Chance Vought. Instead, they continued to ask the Navy what they really wanted in a carrier fighter. They collected a lot of questionnaires from Operations people, BuAer types, and from the CNO. Then they went back to St. Louis and the drawing boards. Within a year they had built a mock-up of what came out of their studies. The Navy was invited to inspect and critique the mock-up. All this additional effort resulted in a letter of intent to design and build two aircraft similar to the mock-up, which was fine ... as far as it went. But there was some feeling around McDonnell that this was little more than a consolation prize for coming in second to the Crusader. This feeling was reinforced by the fact that there was no military requirement for the AH-1, as the Phantom II was then known.

Engineering studies continued, but without a mission requirement to work from design of the fighter was an impossible task. Finally, in April of 1955, the mission was defined by the Navy. It was to be fleet air defense, and the Phantom II would be required to stay on CAP station for three hours. It was to be armed with the latest type of air-to-air missiles, rather than guns. This was not at all what McDonnell had had in mind for their new design. Their AH-1 was a single-place twin engine fighter-bomber, with guns, radar, and 11 external stores stations capable of carrying any ordnance in the Navy arsenal.

The talent and adaptability of the McDonnell design team came to the fore, and within two weeks they had changed the Phantom II into a two place, all-weather interceptor with but one external stores station, (on the centerline for an additional fuel tank) with semi-submerged mountings in the bottom of the fuselage for the new Sparrow AAMs. The revised detail specification was approved by the Navy, and it looked as though the Phantom II might reach production status after all. When this became apparent, the Navy asked Chance Vought to build an airplane that would also fit the selected mission, with the intent of having the two contractors demonstrate their respective designs in a competitive fly-off. Chance Vought built the F8U-3, an uprated version of their successful Crusader. The fly-off took place in 1958, and resulted in a limited production contract for McDonnell.

Project Top Flight Phantom II was F4H-1. Altitude record-setting flight was flown by Cdr. Lawrence E. Flint on December 6, 1959. The flight took 40 minutes from take-off to landing, during which the aircraft assumed a ballistic trajectory near it's peak altitude. With aircraft speed only 45 miles per hour at the top of the trajectory, CDR Flint experienced about a minute and a half of weightlessness. When the flight was done, a new record of 98,557 feet had been established, breaking the Russian record of 94,560 feet set the previous summer in a TU-431. Top Flight was conducted from Edwards AFB. (US Navy)

When the Phantom II set its speed and time to climb records in 1962, it was configured as a regular squadron aircraft, and carried its full complement of fuselage mounted Sparrow missiles. Those records have since been eclipsed by the latest generation of American and Soviet fighters, but they stood for a long time, and are still note-worthy.

TIME TO CLIMB		
Meters	Feet	Seconds
3,000	9,842	34.52
6,000	19,685	48.78
9,000	29,527	61.62
12,000	39.370	77.15
15,000	49,212	114.53
20,000	65,617	178.50
25,000	82,021	230.44
30,000	98,425	371.43

15/25 Kilometer Straightaway	1606 mph
3 Kilometer Low Altitude	920 mph
100 Kilometer Closed Course	1390 mph
500 Kilometer Closed Course	1216 mph
Los Angeles to New York	170 minutes
Sustained Altitude (level flight)	66,443 feet
Altitude	over 100,000 feet

Vintage Phantom II loaded with a large variety of air to ground weapons for the purpose of this static display. First Phantom II's had smaller canopy and nose.

Into Production

Today the performance of the Phantom is somewhat taken for granted, but when it first flew, in 1958, it was stunning! It promised new horizons in fighter tactics, and the first 26 aircraft produced were used to explore the limits of the design. The performance requirements set forth by the Navy were stringent, but the F-4A exceeded them all, as the following chart shows.

System Parameters	Units	Required	Demonstrated
Max power (afterburner)	Mach	2.04	2.03*
Max power (military)	Mach	0.99	1.01
Rate of Climb @ 35,000 feet Max power	ft/min	12,258	17,500
Time to climb to 35,000 feet from S.L. at Max power	min.	1.30	1.13
Time to accelerate from MRT V max to M Max at 35,000 ft.	min.	0.81	0.59
Supersonic combat ceiling with max power	ft.	55,430	56,900
Combat gross weight	lb.	36,817	36,817

*One of the first F-4's, equipped with pre-compressor cooling of water injection, actually reached Mach 2.62 and was still accelerating when the pilot throttled back for fear of what might happen if the water ran out at this speed. The Phantom's redline speed of mach 2.2 is a structural design limit, rather than a true indication of the actual speed potential of the basic design.

F-4 Phantom II Variants

F-4A (F4H-1) First Production version of the Phantom, it was powered by a pair of J-79-GE-2 turbojets. Basic armament consisted of four Sparrow III missiles and an APQ-72 intercept radar. In tests it carried 22 500 pound bombs on fuselage and wing hardpoints. 47 built, of which 26 performed initial testing and development of the design. The remainder were assigned to the first Phantom training squadrons, VF-101 and VF-121.

F-4B (F4H-1F) 649 produced, from 1961 through 1966. The first large scale production version of the Phantom, powered by the uprated J-79-GE-8 engines, which gave 10,900 lbs thrust in military and 17,000 lbs thrust in afterburner. Also equipped with the AJB-3A bombing system and capable of carrying up to 16,000 lbs of ordnance on five hardpoints. Total internal fuel capacity was 2,000 gallons. Retained the APQ-72 fire control system and was equipped with AAA-4 infra-red sensor under nose for use with Sidewinder missiles. Could carry six Sparrows, or four Sparrows and four Sidewinders.

RF-4B (F4H-1P) Developed for the U.S. Marine Corps, it had dual controls deleted and carried reconnaissance equipment. First flight was in March, 1965. A total of 46 were built.

F-4C (F-110A) First of the U.S. Air Force Phantoms, it was developed from the F-4B. Principle changes included the addition of an inertial navigation system, larger tires and brakes, updated APQ-100 radar, and dual controls. Powered by J-79-GE-15 engines, equipped with cartridge starters. It was built for interdiction and air superiority role, rather than intercept role originally intended for the Navy's Phantom. First flew on 27 May, 1963. 583 delivered to USAF through 1966, of which 36 were eventually supplied to the Spanish Air Force. Has also served with the Air National Guard since 1972. Two squadrons currently operating F-4C in the Wild Weasel defense suppression role, carrying ECM warning sensors, jamming pods, chaff dispensers, and anti-radiation missiles.

RF-4C (RF-110A) First of the RF Phantom variants, first flight was on 9 August, 1963. Radar and photographic systems are housed in a modified nose which adds 33 inches to the overall basic length of the Phantom. Three basic recce systems, which are operated from the rear seat, comprise side-looking radar, an infrared sensor and forward and side looking cameras. Has operated with ANG since 1972. Total production through 1973 was 505.

F-4D Developed from the F-4C. Major systems changes introduced, including APQ-109 fire-control radar, ASG-22 sight, ASQ-91 weapons release computer, ASG-22 lead computing amplifier and lead computing gyro, and ASN-63 inertial navigation system. First flight on 8 December, 1965. Production deliveries began in March, 1966. Total of 843 built, of which 32 supplied to Imperial Iranian Air Force, and 18 to Republic of Korea Air Force.

F-4E Developed as an improvement in the F-4D, the principle change being the addition of the M-61A1 Vulcan cannon under the nose, it also carries an improved fire-control system, an additional fuselage fuel cell, and current models are being retro-fitted with the leading edge maneuvering slats developed for the F-4F wing. Also being re-equipped with Northrop target identification system electro-optical, which is a form of TV camera with zoom lens, which greatly aides in long-range visual identification of targets. Current improvements also include Pave Tack system, which provides a day/night all-weather capability to acquire, track, and designate ground targets for laser, infrared, and electro-optically guided weapons. First production version delivered to USAF in 1967. Also supplied to Israel, Iran, Greece, Turkey, and loaned to Australia pending deliveries of their F-111's. Israeli F-4E's will be retro-fitted with leading edge maneuvering slats.

RF-4E Built for the West German Luftwaffe and Japan. It is essentially the same as the RF-4C, with the exception of uprated J-79-GE-17 engines, and slightly different recce equipment. 88 built for Germany, 14 for Japan.

F-4EJ License built version of the USAF F-4E for the Japan Air Self Defense Force. First two were built by McDonnell Douglas, the remaining 102 to be built by the Japanese. Specialized equipment includes tail warning radar and provision for firing the Mitsubishi AAM-2 missiles. First flight January, 1971.

F-4F Latest version of the Phantom, developed for the West German Luftwaffe, which has ordered 175. It is basically the same as the F-4E, with these exceptions: Leading Edge maneuvering slats on the wings, non-slotted stabilator ala RF-4C, AIM-9E Sidewinders and Vulcan nose cannon are primary armament, with Sparrow and Falcon missile capabilities deleted. Provisions for air-to-ground weapons carriage incorporated to provide secondary capability for ground support missions.

F-4G Two versions of the F-4G have existed. Twelve F-4B's were modified during production with AN/ASW-21 data link communications equipment. They served with VF-213, onboard USS Kitty Hawk in late 1965. Latest version to carry F-4G designation is a modified F-4E airframe, with extensive electronic warfare system, which will operate in the Wild Weasel mission.

F-4J A follow-on development of the F-4B for the Navy and Marine Corps, the F-4J first flew in 1966. Over 500 built before end of production run. Continued primary role of interceptor, but with full ground attack capability. Also introduced drooped ailerons and slotted stabilator for lower carrier approach speeds and enhanced low speed handling. Powered by J-79-GE-10 engines with 17,900 lbs thrust with afterburner.

F-4K Development of the F-4J for the Royal Navy, included several major changes. Powered by more powerful Rolls Royce Spey RB 168-25R Turbofans, which dictated enlarging of intakes laterally by 6 inches. Smaller British carriers dictated shortening of aircraft through the use of a foldable radome so that Phantom would fit on elevators. Nose strut extends 40 inches (vice 20 inches on F-4J) to allow for optimum angle of attack at launch. First flight on 27 June, 1966. 24 ordered as Phantom FG Mk 1. Employs Martin-Baker ejection seats and carries Sparrow missiles.

F-4M Similar to F-4K, but with provisions for land based operations with RAF. 170 ordered as Phantom FGR Mk 2. Built by McDonnell Douglas, but with 50% of components manufactured in the United Kingdom. First flight in February, 1967. Both the F-4K and F-4M carry a reconnaissance pod which is similar in shape to the standard U.S. 600 gallon centerline drop tank.

F-4N Result of an update program conducted by Naval Air Rework Facility, NAS North Island, under the project name "Bee-Line". 178 older F-4B's, selected from blocks 12 through 28, on the basis of accelerometer data, number of catapult launches, number of arrestments, and hours remaining before completion of service life, were put through this program beginning in 1971. F-4N project incorporated in-depth structural modifications to improve aircraft fatigue life, added a 60-kva power generating system and replaced wiring and connectors to achieve a standard electrical configuration, and updated avionics systems to improve air combat maneuvering capabilities. The updating gives F-4N crews automatic altitude reporting (AIMS), data link, air-to-air IFF, visual target acquisition system (VTAS), Sidewinder expanded capabilities (SEAM), dogfight computer, pilot lock-on mode, and electronic countermeasures (ECM) improvements. F-4N has every outstanding Navy F-4 change, making it roughly equivalent to latest operational fleet F-4B, and assures fleet service into the eighties.

F-4J/S Leading edge slats and a modified engine are major improvements planned for 260 F-4J aircraft that will be modified to F-4S standard beginning in the spring of 1978. Also in the modification package are new wiring, pneumatic and hydraulic tubing, and structural improvements, all designed to add 10 years to the service life of the aircraft. The modified engine is the low-smoke, long-life J79-GE-10B. An improved weapons control system, designated AN/AWG-10A, will also be installed.

F-4 Development

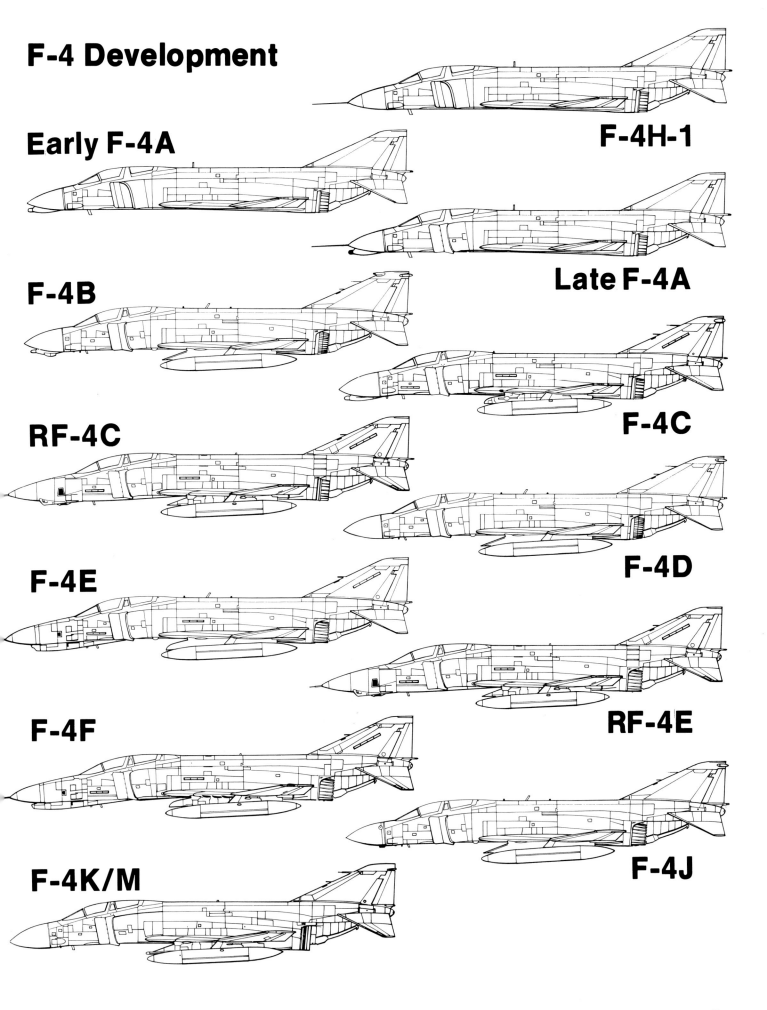

F-4H-1

Early F-4A

Late F-4A

F-4B

F-4C

RF-4C

F-4D

F-4E

RF-4E

F-4F

F-4J

F-4K/M

F-4E

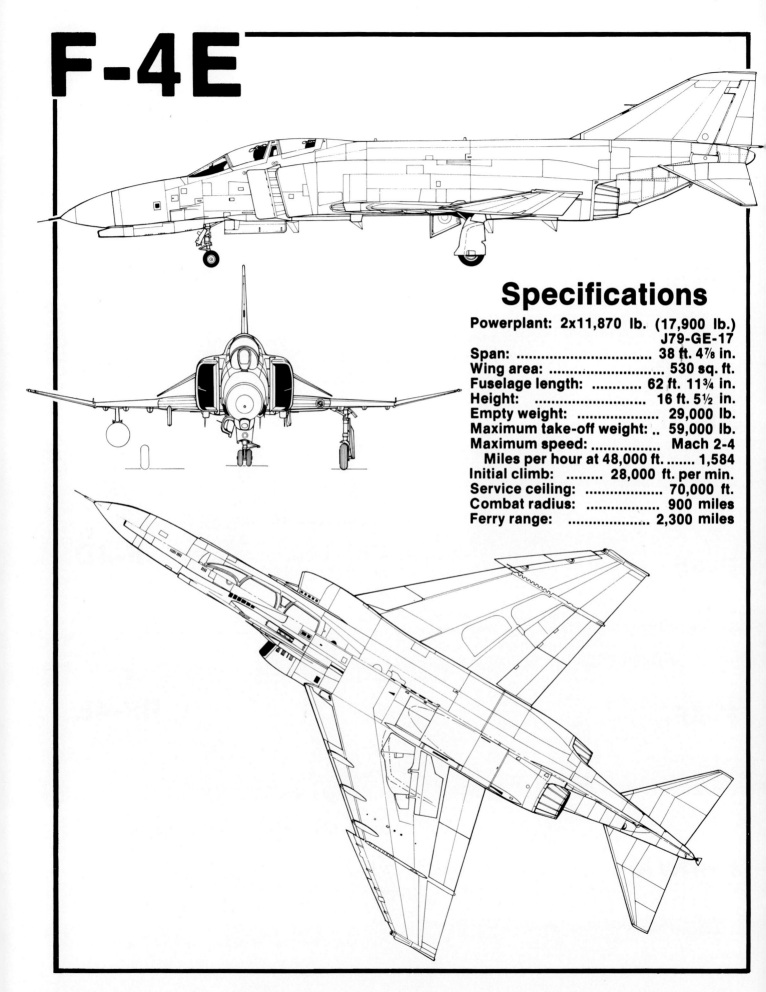

Specifications

Powerplant: 2x11,870 lb. (17,900 lb.)
J79-GE-17
Span: .... 38 ft. 4⅞ in.
Wing area: .... 530 sq. ft.
Fuselage length: .... 62 ft. 11¾ in.
Height: .... 16 ft. 5½ in.
Empty weight: .... 29,000 lb.
Maximum take-off weight: .. 59,000 lb.
Maximum speed: .... Mach 2-4
   Miles per hour at 48,000 ft. 1,584
Initial climb: .... 28,000 ft. per min.
Service ceiling: .... 70,000 ft.
Combat radius: .... 900 miles
Ferry range: .... 2,300 miles

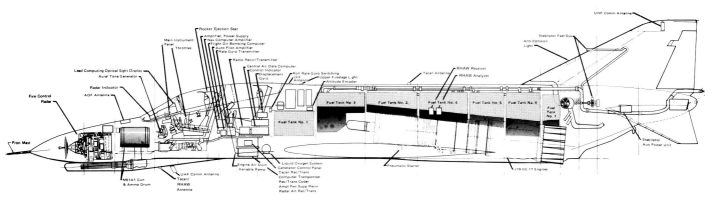

F-4 Equipment Arrangement

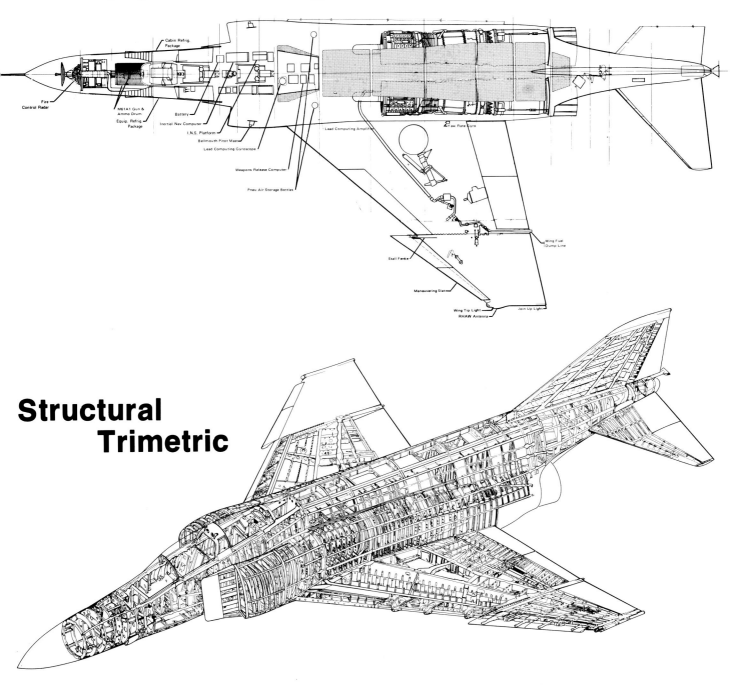

Structural Trimetric

AF 65 830

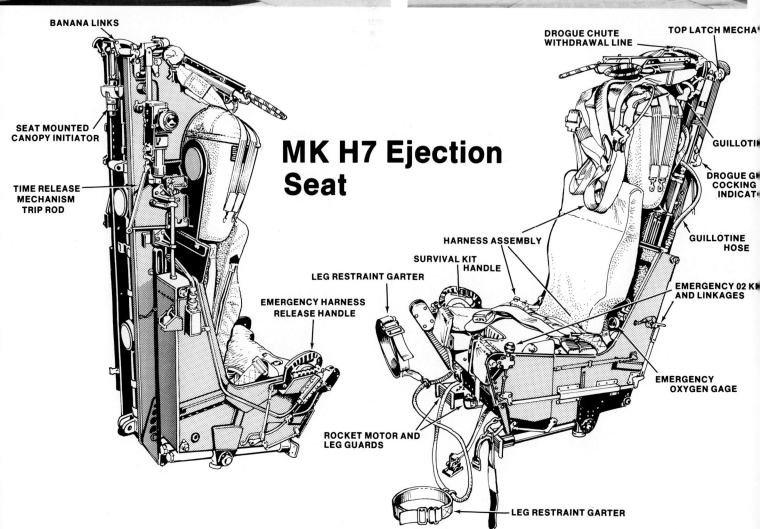

MK H7 Ejection Seat

BANANA LINKS

SEAT MOUNTED
CANOPY INITIATOR

TIME RELEASE
MECHANISM
TRIP ROD

EMERGENCY HARNESS
RELEASE HANDLE

LEG RESTRAINT GARTER

EMERGENCY HARNESS
RELEASE HANDLE

ROCKET MOTOR AND
LEG GUARDS

DROGUE CHUTE
WITHDRAWAL LINE

TOP LATCH MECHA

GUILLOTI

DROGUE G
COCKING
INDICAT

GUILLOTINE
HOSE

HARNESS ASSEMBLY

SURVIVAL KIT
HANDLE

EMERGENCY 02 K
AND LINKAGES

EMERGENCY
OXYGEN GAGE

LEG RESTRAINT GARTER

F-4C Front Cockpit Arrangement

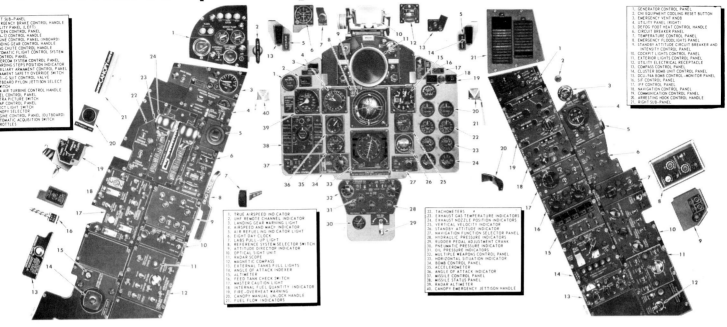

LEFT SUB-PANEL
1. EMERGENCY BRAKE CONTROL HANDLE
2. UTILITY PANEL (LEFT)
3. OXYGEN CONTROL PANEL
4. ENGINE CONTROL HANDLE
5. CM-12 CONTROL PANEL (INBOARD)
6. LANDING GEAR CONTROL HANDLE
7. DRAG CHUTE CONTROL HANDLE
8. AUTOMATIC FLIGHT CONTROL SYSTEM CONTROL PANEL
9. INTERCOM SYSTEM CONTROL PANEL
10. BOARDING STEPS POSITION INDICATOR
11. AUXILIARY ARMAMENT CONTROL PANEL
12. EXHAUST SAFETY OVERRIDE SWITCH
13. ANTI-G SUIT TURBINE CONTROL HANDLE
14. OUTBOARD PYLON JETTISON SELECT SWITCH
15. RAM AIR TURBINE CONTROL HANDLE
16. FUEL CONTROL PANEL
17. FLAP CONTROL PANEL
18. EXTRA PICTURE SWITCH
19. EJECT LIGHT SWITCH
20. CANOPY SELECTOR
21. ENGINE CONTROL PANEL (OUTBOARD)
22. AUTOMATIC ACQUISITION SWITCH
23. THROTTLES

1. TRUE AIRSPEED INDICATOR
2. UHF REMOTE CHANNEL INDICATOR
3. LANDING GEAR WARNING LIGHT
4. AIRSPEED AND MACH INDICATOR
5. AIR REFUELING INDICATOR LIGHT
6. EIGHT DAY CLOCK
7. LABS PULL-UP LIGHT
8. REFERENCE SYSTEM SELECTOR SWITCH
9. ATTITUDE DIRECTOR INDICATOR
10. OPTICAL SIGHT UNIT
11. RADAR SCOPE
12. MAGNETIC COMPASS
13. EXTERNAL TANKS FULL LIGHTS
14. ANGLE OF ATTACK INDEXER
15. ALTIMETER
16. FEED TANK CHECK SWITCH
17. MASTER CAUTION LIGHT
18. INTERNAL FUEL QUANTITY INDICATOR
19. FIRE-OVERHEAT WARNING
20. CANOPY MANUAL UNLOCK HANDLE
21. FUEL FLOW INDICATORS

22. TACHOMETERS
23. EXHAUST GAS TEMPERATURE INDICATORS
24. EXHAUST NOZZLE POSITION INDICATORS
25. VERTICAL VELOCITY INDICATOR
26. STANDBY ATTITUDE INDICATOR
27. NAVIGATION FUNCTION SELECTOR PANEL
28. HYDRAULIC PRESSURE INDICATORS
29. RUDDER PEDAL ADJUSTMENT CRANK
30. PNEUMATIC PRESSURE INDICATOR
31. OIL PRESSURE INDICATORS
32. MULTIPLE WEAPONS CONTROL PANEL
33. HORIZONTAL SITUATION INDICATOR
34. BOMB CONTROL PANEL
35. ACCELEROMETER
36. ANGLE OF ATTACK INDICATOR
37. MISSILE CONTROL PANEL
38. MISSILE STATUS PANEL
39. RADAR ALTIMETER
40. CANOPY EMERGENCY JETTISON HANDLE

1. GENERATOR CONTROL PANEL
2. CNI EQUIPMENT COOLING RESET BUTTON
3. EMERGENCY VENT KNOB
4. UTILITY PANEL (RIGHT)
5. DEFOG FOOT HEAT CONTROL HANDLE
6. CIRCUIT BREAKER PANEL
7. TEMPERATURE CONTROL PANEL
8. EMERGENCY FLOODLIGHTS PANEL
9. STANDBY ATTITUDE CIRCUIT BREAKER AND INTENSITY CONTROL PANEL
10. COCKPIT LIGHTS CONTROL PANEL
11. EXTERIOR LIGHTS CONTROL PANEL
12. UTILITY ELECTRICAL RECEPTACLE
13. COMPASS CONTROL PANEL
14. CLUSTER BOMB UNIT CONTROL PANEL
15. DCU-R4A BOMB CONTROL-MONITOR PANEL
16. SIF CONTROL PANEL
17. IFF CONTROL PANEL
18. NAVIGATION CONTROL PANEL
19. COMMUNICATION CONTROL PANEL
20. ARRESTING HOOK CONTROL HANDLE
21. RIGHT SUB-PANEL

Rear Cockpit Arrangement

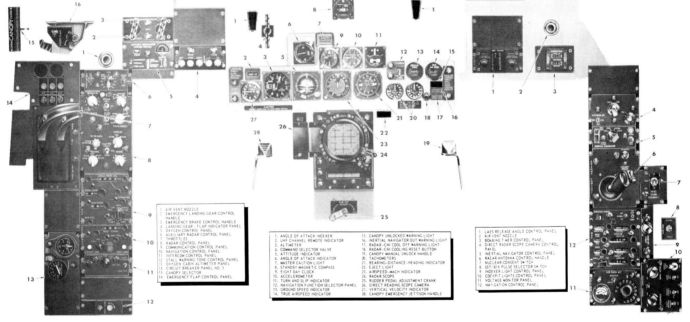

1. AIR VENT NOZZLE
2. EMERGENCY LANDING GEAR CONTROL HANDLE
3. EMERGENCY BRAKE CONTROL HANDLE
4. LANDING GEAR-FLAP INDICATOR PANEL
5. OXYGEN CONTROL PANEL
6. AUXILIARY RADAR CONTROL PANEL
7. THROTTLES
8. RADAR CONTROL PANEL
9. COMMUNICATION CONTROL PANEL
10. NAVIGATION CONTROL PANEL
11. INTERCOM CONTROL PANEL
12. STALL WARNING TONE CONTROL PANEL
13. OXYGEN CABIN ALTIMETER PANEL
14. CIRCUIT BREAKER PANEL NO. 3
15. CANOPY SELECTOR
16. EMERGENCY FLAP CONTROL PANEL

1. ANGLE OF ATTACK INDEXER
2. UHF CHANNEL, REMOTE INDICATOR
3. ALTIMETER
4. COMMAND SELECTOR VALVE
5. ATTITUDE INDICATOR
6. ANGLE OF ATTACK INDICATOR
7. MASTER CAUTION LIGHT
8. STANDBY MAGNETIC COMPASS
9. EIGHT DAY CLOCK
10. ACCELEROMETER
11. TURN AND SLIP INDICATOR
12. NAVIGATION FUNCTION SELECTOR PANEL
13. GROUND SPEED INDICATOR
14. TRUE AIRSPEED INDICATOR
15. CANOPY UNLOCKED WARNING LIGHT
16. INERTIAL NAVIGATOR OUT WARNING LIGHT
17. RADAR-CNI COOL OFF WARNING LIGHT
18. RADAR-CNI COOLING RESET BUTTON
19. CANOPY MANUAL UNLOCK HANDLE
20. TACHOMETERS
21. BEARING-DISTANCE-HEADING INDICATOR
22. EJECT LIGHT
23. AIRSPEED-MACH INDICATOR
24. RADAR SCOPE
25. RUDDER PEDAL ADJUSTMENT CRANK
26. DIRECT READING SCOPE CAMERA
27. VERTICAL VELOCITY INDICATOR
28. CANOPY EMERGENCY JETTISON HANDLE

1. LABS RELEASE ANGLE CONTROL PANEL
2. AIR VENT NOZZLE
3. BOMBING TIMER CONTROL PANEL
4. DIRECT RADAR SCOPE CAMERA CONTROL PANEL
5. INERTIAL NAVIGATOR CONTROL PANEL
6. RADAR ANTENNA CONTROL HANDLE
7. NUCLEAR CONSENT SWITCH
8. SST-181X PULSE SELECTOR SWITCH
9. INDEXER LIGHT CONTROL PANEL
10. COCKPIT LIGHTS CONTROL PANEL
11. VOLTAGE MONITOR PANEL
12. NAVIGATION CONTROL PANEL

Front Cockpit Control Stick

Rear Cockpit Control Stick

Phantom Weapons

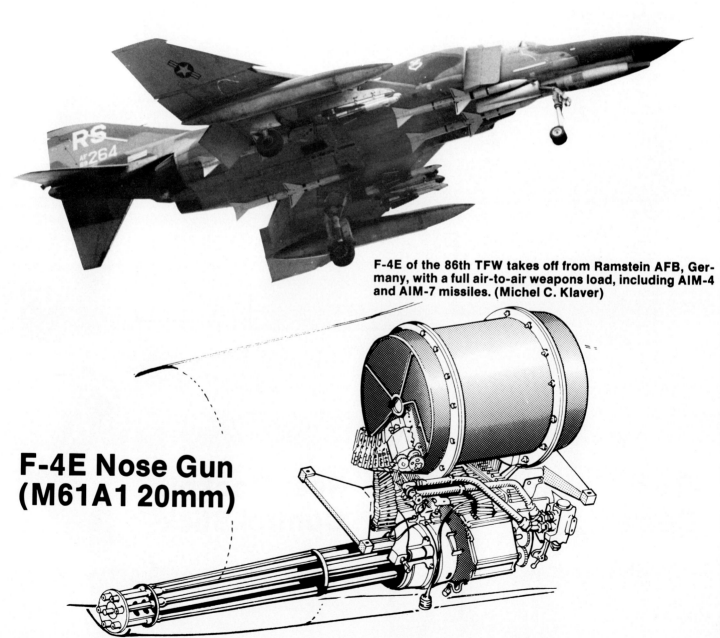

F-4E of the 86th TFW takes off from Ramstein AFB, Germany, with a full air-to-air weapons load, including AIM-4 and AIM-7 missiles. (Michel C. Klaver)

F-4E Nose Gun (M61A1 20mm)

Centerline Rack and MER

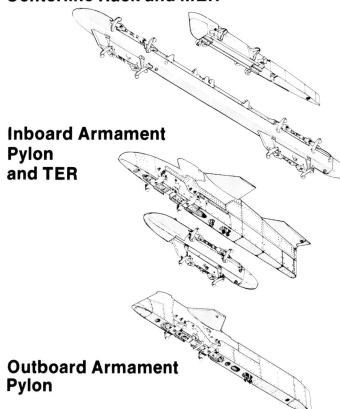

Inboard Armament Pylon and TER

Outboard Armament Pylon

(Above left) 750 pound bombs on outboard wing pylon. (Ken Buchanan)

Triple Ejector Rack (TER) loaded on inboard pylon carries three Mark 84's. (USAF)

Loading 500 pound bombs on centerline multiple ejector rack (MER). Note strike camera carried in starboard forward missile well. (Norman E. Taylor)

Normal Release Sequence

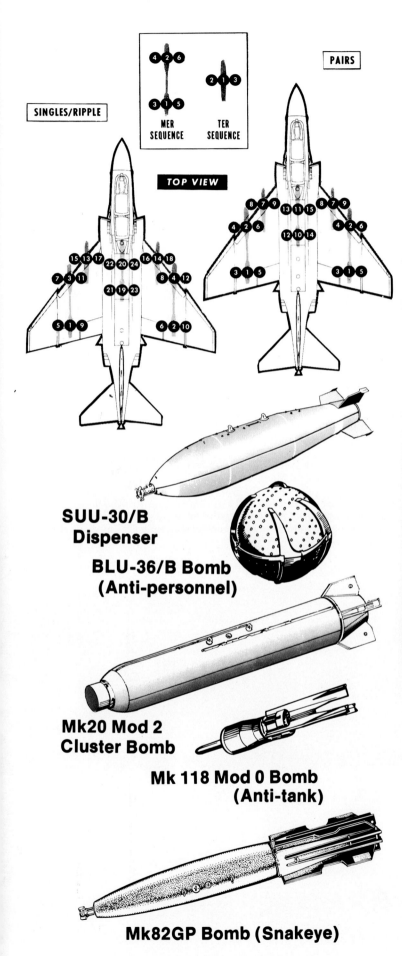

SINGLES/RIPPLE

PAIRS

MER SEQUENCE

TER SEQUENCE

TOP VIEW

SUU-30/B Dispenser

BLU-36/B Bomb (Anti-personnel)

Mk20 Mod 2 Cluster Bomb

Mk 118 Mod 0 Bomb (Anti-tank)

Mk82GP Bomb (Snakeye)

AIM-9 Sidewinder missiles being wheeled to Phantom by a red shirt aboard carrier in Gulf of Tonkin. Missiles have protective covers installed over heat-seekers in noses. (US Navy)

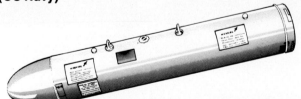

LAU-59/A Rocket Launcher

2.75" FFAR

14

KMV-351/B Laser Guided Bomb (MK84 LGB)

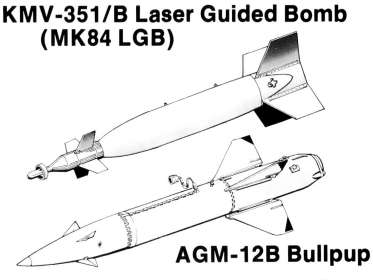

AGM-12B Bullpup

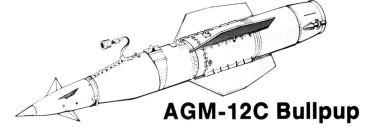

AGM-12C Bullpup

(Left & Left Above) Pave Spike pod installed on port forward Sparrow missile well of F-4D "Smart Bomber". (USAF)

Pave Knife Pod on inboard wing pylon of F-4D. This Pod is used as the laser designator which allows laser-guided bombs to home on target. (USAF)

F-4B of VF-84 aboard USS Independence being hooked to catapult. (US Navy)

The Navy & the Phantom

Lieutenant Commander Dan Macintyre was credited with the fourth MIG kill for the U.S. Navy in the Vietnam war. It was the fifth kill for a Phantom crew in the war, and came as a result of the first MIG engagement in what was then a ten-month long cruise on "Yankee Station".

Dan Macintyre's training and experience for his "moment of truth" was extensive and varied. He had started his flying career in SNJ's, then on to T-28's, T-33's, and F9F-2 Panthers, before graduating to a regular squadron. In 1956 he was assigned to VF-111 at N.A.S. Alameda, where he flew the F9F-8 Cougar. In 1957, VF-111 switched to the FJ-3M Fury. It was during the last cruise of the Bennington as a CVA (Attack Carrier), while he was flying the Fury, that he saw his first MIG's. During the time when the Chinese Communists were shelling the islands of Quemoy and Matsu, and the U.S. Navy was flexing its muscles in the straits of Formosa as a response. Regular air patrols were flown and on one of these, several MIG-15's were spotted. They stayed on their side of the line and the Furies remained on their side. It was an exciting, if irrelevant, incident in the life of a young fighter pilot.

Upon completion of this cruise, he was assigned to VF-124 at N.A.S. Moffett Field where he flew the F9F-8T for a year as an instrument instructor. He was then assigned as a fighter combat tactics instructor in the F-8 for another year.

In November of 1960 he was assigned to VT-24 at N.A.A.S. Chase Field, Texas. He had applied for assignment to the U.S. Navy Flight Demonstration Team, Blue Angels previously, and before he had a chance to settle into his duties at Chase, he was given the Christmas present all fighter pilots dream of ... acceptance to that elite group of aviators that have become famous throughout the world. Dan flew the F-11 Tiger for three years as a member of the Blues, the first year as solo, then two years as right wing in the "Diamond". He then reported to VF-121, the Pacific fleet RAG (Replacement Aircrew Training Group) squadron at N.A.S. Miramar, California in January of 1964. His narrative recalling his experiences and impressions of the F-4 Phantom are the highlight of this book.

"As you know, the F-4 was designed and built as a fleet defense interceptor. Perhaps because of this mission, the first people to fly it when it came into the Navy were what I'll call, "night fighters". They were all-weather pilots who had cut their fighter teeth on the F2H Banshee and F3H Demon. The Demon was a ... mistake. The airplane started off on good footing from an aerodynamic standpoint, but because of engine availability problems during its production, it wound up being a grossly underpowered machine. As such, the pilots who flew it found it most prudent to concern themselves with interceptor tactics, and almost never seriously concerned themselves with day, clear air mass, air superiority fighter tactics. Now, when those folks got into the Phantom, they didn't appreciably change their tactics, especially since they now were flying an aircraft designed specifically for what they had been doing all along. Well, when the inevitable hassles between F-8's and F-4's occurred, (Author's note: It is well to remember here that the F8U-3 had lost out to the F-4 in the D.O.D. "fly-off" competition and any Crusader jock worth his salt was not going to pass up an opportunity to prove the wrong airplane had been selected.) the F-4 always came out second best. Not because the Phantom was necessarily the inferior fighter, but rather because at that time the people driving them didn't understand air combat tactics well enough to fight their way out of a wet paper sack. The Crusader gang, on the other hand, lived with those tactics as a way of life. The night fighter types were intimately familiar with tactics necessary to go after a basically non-maneuvering target, such as a bomber, with a standard missile attack and reattack. But that was generally about as aggressive as their missions got.

When I arrived at the RAG in 1964, I heard many many stories from both the Crusader pilots who had hassled against the Phantom and the

LCDR Dan Macintyre strapping in prior to August 1966 mission over North Vietnam.

Phantom pilots who had tried. According to just about everybody, the Phantom was simply another lump of lead like the Demon, only faster and possessed with a better rate of climb because of the two J-79's it hauled around. Based on adventures resulting from nearly three years of fleet experience with the F-4, it was easily beaten in a dogfight, a real "piece of cake". There were a couple of Phantom pilots at that time who insisted the machine was really OK. However, with all the Crusader pilots in agreement about the F-4's rotten air-to-air showing and the vast majority of F-4 drivers nodding their heads, what fool was to believe the wishful tales of the few who spoke up for the poor Phantom. When I finished the ground school and finally got to fly the plane, I was impressed that it didn't seem to handle that much differently than other fighters, including the Crusader, that I had experience with. At that time I had something over 3,000 hours of fighter time ... all primarily concerned with day, clear air mass, air combat tactics.

One day early in my F-4 training, I was cruising around in my Phantom when I spotted a lone Crusader about the same time he saw me and we had at one another. It was one of those nice engagements where both planes started even ... head on ... co-altitude ... no holds barred. We had three engagements and I wound up at his "six" each time. Although I had to work pretty hard to gain the final advantage on this fellow, I sort of figured he didn't really know how to fight the Crusader "hard," because according to all I had heard, he should have been able to have me in six delicious flavors. Just to check on it though, I picked off the squadron and aircraft number of the F-8 and made a phone call when I got back on the ground. The pilot of the Crusader turned out to be an old roommate of mine from my days as an F-8 air combat instructor. Lt. Dave Morris was one fine fighter driver! ... and I had just discovered something important about the Phantom!

After that, we really started to dig into the issue, and we found some pretty encouraging data on the Phantom as it compared to other aircraft. The Crusader had greater instantaneous "G" capability, but the Phantom had the greater sustained "G" and energy capability. What this meant, of course, was that if you could avoid losing the fight in the first turn, you could pretty well control what happened from that point on. This was a direct result of the F-4's tremendous power, or thrust-to-weight ratio, which allowed us to maintain higher sustained "G" and energy levels than the Crusader and most other aircraft we could expect to come up against in a fight. From that point on, given pilots of equal ability, the Phantom seldom lost a fight to the Crusader. I might mention, at this point, that we paid dearly for this advantage. All that engine power

working against the F-4's great weight and relatively high wing loading, didn't come free. An enormous amount of fuel was consumed by those J-79's in the process. The pilot who didn't fully appreciate this fact allowing himself to get carried away with the excitement of a good hard fight and forgetting prudent fuel management, was going to find himself perhaps the victor of a fight, but without sufficient fuel to get his precious Phantom home. Recalling the skies over North Vietnam, I don't remember offhand the exact economics of swapping a MIG you shot down with a Phantom you lost on the way home due to fuel starvation, but it was strongly in the enemy's favor. The really good Phantom fighter drivers became masters at the fuel management game. While we are talking about day fighter tactics, I think it is most necessary to mention one of the great disadvantages almost all of our U. S. machines had when compared to the MIGs. Simply stated, our engines smoked, theirs didn't. This was a very serious detriment, and one of which we were acutely aware when we went over North Vietnam on business. During many training missions, which involved other F-4's or A-4, A-6, and F-8 aircraft, I might never have seen the plane I was going after, but at extreme distances I could pick up the smoke trail, and I knew if I followed it long enough, I would eventually be able to spot the guy. You've got to know that if I was able to take advantage of this tactical fault, the North Vietnamese surely could do it. The records show, they often did.

My idea of the classic air superiority fighter is a small smokeless aircraft with extremely high levels of acceleration and deceleration capability, very agile or maneuverable, with absolutely superior visibility out of the cockpit through all dimensions, and a reasonable weapons mix for the job at hand. I would say that the outcome of a jet dogfight depends ... up to 85% ... on being able to see your opponent more than he gets to see you during the fight. When you consider a "turning" fight in a combat area, chances are mighty good that you will start the fight with your speed up. The fight will be over quickly, since nobody fools around much during those things. Get your kills as swiftly as possible, without the dazzling slow speed aerial trickery that made you the toast of the Miramar Officer's Saloon. The longest fights I heard of in North Vietnam didn't go over two minutes, so you'll probably keep your speed level pretty well up throughout the contest. At any speeds we're talking about, the diameter of that circle you are fighting in might be up to four miles. When you consider that five miles is generally the maximum distance you can see a fighter-size target, and it's tough then, and that you really can't distinguish details until you're within a couple miles, you can easily appreciate the bad disadvantages of being in a big, smokey airplane.

From VF-121, I was assigned to VF-151, as assistant operations officer. I happened to be the only guy in that squadron who had any honest training or experience in clear air mass fighter tactics, so I was the logical fellow to write the criteria on fighter tactics for the squadron. These were later adopted as standard for the Air Wing also. On our first cruise, in Coral Sea (CVA-43), VF-154 was our sister fighter squadron and they were still flying Crusaders. We worked out a set of tactics that allowed us to use both fighter squadrons in the same airspace, in fact, in the same formations, which maximized use of the Phantom's superior air-to-air radar, and the Crusader's great initial maneuverability.

Of course, I wasn't the only guy who was finding out that the Phantom was going to work well in the air superiority role. While I was working out tactics in VF-151, Lt. Sam Flynn was introducing some new wrinkles into the VF-121 training syllabus. But all of this, with inputs from many good aerial warfare tacticians who were now finding their way into the F-4 community was the beginning of the Phantom's role as a mainstay air superiority fighter. It's interesting to note that as a result of these new tactics we worked out, VF-151 was the only squadron in the Air Wing to engage in combat throughout two cruises, (over a 16 month period) on a day to day basis, without losing a single airplane or aircrew to enemy action.

On that first cruise, only about 20% of the missions we flew were fighter oriented. These were missions on which we carried a weapons compliment comprised entirely of air-to-air Sparrow or Sidewinder missiles and acted as either BARCAP (Barrier Combat Air Patrol) TARCAP (Target Combat Air Patrol) or RECCE (Reconnaissance) escort. On the balance of our missions, we were loaded with a variety of bombs or air-to-ground rockets, and briefed for flak suppression duties. On these missions we would accompany the strike force into the target area, and usually roll in on the target positions first. If we drew fire from AAA (Anti-Aircraft Artillery), we would then concentrate on their positions while the tactical bombers took care of the briefed target. We often had pre-briefed AAA or SAM (Surface-to-Air Missile) we were to told to hit or watch for, but the North Vietnamese, being a cagey lot, would more often than not, move those sites around. At least, they did until the latter stages of the war. Then they had so much AAA in North Vietnam, there wasn't any place they could move an AAA battery that wasn't already full of guns, and virtually the same was true of the SAM sites.

We were learning a lot more about the Phantom. Remember, it had started life as a pure interceptor. We discovered it would make a fairly acceptable air superiority fighter in skilled hands. Now we were to learn about its air-to-ground weapons delivery capabilities, which turned out to be formidable. You have to come back and give some more credit to the phenominal power generated by those twin J-79's. After all, the F-4 shouldn't have even made a fair fighter as it had a wing loading of 87 pounds per square foot with 60% of its fuel remaining. That's twenty pounds more than the wing loading of the MIG 21 under the same conditions and just twenty less than a missile! Now, in the air-to-ground role, the F-4 could carry more ordnance than a World War II four engine bomber! When we first went to war with the F-4, we had sections in the manual detailing how we could carry a wide variety of ordnance loads. We had done some air-to-ground work with training equipment during the pre-deployment phase, and each aircrew in the squadron had even been able to drop at least a couple of real Mk. 80 series bombs on the California or Nevada desert. Being a younger, somewhat pragmatic officer in those days, and basically a fighter purist, I secretly hoped the air-to-ground mission, which naturally entailed carriage of a lot of high drag, performance degrading hardware, would go away like a bad dream. But it took the same war I hoped would allow the fighter to emerge in full glory to show me the Navy was indeed serious about hanging a bunch of junk on this beautiful airplane.

We went through some ragged learning experiences with our Phantoms and the air-to-ground war. In 1965, when we first went over to Vietnam in Coral Sea, about 30% of the ordnance loads the aircraft could carry with the existing carriage equipment were not approved loads because the Navy hadn't finished evaluating the engineering and safety aspects. So we started off behind the power curve. As an example of the virtual pioneer work many of our Phantom people did to make it an effective air-to-ground warplane; One problem that cropped up early, was the inability to carry any missiles on the two inboard wing ordnance stations when bombs or rocket pods were carried on those stations. This was a serious problem because many missions were flown as flak suppression into "MIG Country" and the F-4's were expected to provide TARCAP after delivering their air-to-ground ordnance. We could always hang Sparrows on the fuselage missile stations, but those inboard wing stations were the only place we could carry our infra-red seeking Sidewinders! A couple of ingenious souls in VF-24 came up with a "field solution" to the problem by manufacturing extended missile launcher mounting bolts which effectively moved the Sidewinder launch rails out beyond the bomb load hung directly underneath it. The squadron ran some abbreviated local tests on the whole affair, off and on the carrier, decided it would work, and used the modified equipment on a limited basis until formal approval could be obtained from our Naval Weapons people in the United States. It was quite awhile before approval was finally official. In the meantime, those modified bolts were boot-legged through every F-4 squadron in the combat area and more were manufactured in the machine shops. They were used because they solved a thorny problem and fortunately, as was later proven by controlled testing, it was a good solution. By and large, the basic equipment for the F-4 air-to-ground mission was on its way when the Phantom went to war, but there were quite a few "field fixes" developed out of necessity on the carriers in the combat zone. Most of these "on-the-spot" developments were ideas of our very resourceful junior officers and enlisted personnel.

Stablemates. F-4B of VF-102 being readied for launch from forward cat of Enterprise, as RF-8 of VFP-62 is launched from waist cat, circa 1963. (US Navy)

LCDR Macintyre next to VF-151 CO's airplane. Cdr. J.J. Chambers was prematurely gray, hence the name "gray eagle" on the splitter vane.

My MIG kill came on 6 October 1965. We had been out on the cruise about ten months, without ever seeing any MIGs. Ironically, I was not even supposed to launch on this mission. When the squadron had aircraft scheduled for a mission, we would start up a spare on the flight deck, just in case one of the primary airplanes had a mechanical problem and couldn't launch. I was sitting in the spare, when the number two F-4 went "down" on the deck and couldn't make the launch. I taxied to the cat, launched, and joined up on the flight leader, LCDR Tom Ewall. Tom was our maintenance officer, and by experience, a night fighter pilot. He had been a Demon pilot and was not versed in, nor did he show much interest in learning, clear air mass fighter tactics.

My airplane was configured with three Sparrows (AIM-7D) and two Sidewinders (AIM-9B). I was carrying the 600 centerline fuel tank as well.

Our mission was to act as BARCAP for ten A-4's that were striking the Vu Chua railroad and highway bridge, which was north of Hanoi, and led to China. It was one of the vital links in the North Vietnamese supply chain. We knew that the North Vietnamese had at least a half dozen MIG-17's at Kep Airfield, plus an unknown number of MIG-17 and 21 aircraft at Phuc Yen, about 20 miles from us. We were not allowed to hit Phuc Yen, but Kep was not on the "off-limits" list, So, a simultaneous strike of A-4's was put on it. Four F-8's from VF-154 were to act as TARCAP for the Kep strike.

We went "feet dry" at Cam Pha, and proceeded directly west with our strike group of A-4's. The bridge we were to strike was about ten miles west of Kep, and when we got to it, we ran into an incredible amount of AAA fire. It was such a vital link for the North Vietnamese that they really had it well defended, and only crazy folks would fly over it ... we did,

VF-143 F-4B with everything out approaches Constellation for landing. (US Navy)

which lets you know a lot about your basic fighter pilot.

The weather in the target area was great for a picnic. Bright sunshine, puffy white clouds that were scattered to broken at about 3,000 feet with the tops of them about 4,500 feet ... visibility under the clouds, ten miles plus. We set up our orbit at about 2,500 feet and were bubbling along at something like 450 knots. Our strike group was on Red Crown frequency (the code name for a cruiser in the Gulf of Tonkin supplying GCI information), but because of the range and our low altitude, we were not receiving any of their transmissions. The other strike group was on a different frequency, so we had no contact with them. We did pick up the F-8's on our radar occasionally though, and we knew it was them from watching the pattern they flew.

We picked up the MIGs on our radar when they were about 18 miles south, and closing. At the time, for some reason, we both thought we were looking at the F-8 TARCAP, but for lack of any other action, and just out of common sense, we tracked them as they approached, and began to work ourselves into a more favorable attack position. We had been flying roughly line-abreast formation, with 2,000 feet separating our aircraft. I slid back about a mile to give a better position for an intercept. At eight miles range, my RIO, LTJG Al Johnson, achieved a lock-on with the number two plane in what was now showing up as a three plane line-astern formation. We were quite suspicious, this definitely wasn't an F-8 formation.

At about three miles range, I picked them up visually and broadcast the call: "Three MIG-17's, on the nose!" They were heading about 040 degrees, crossing right to left in front of us, altitude about 3,000 feet and doing maybe 250 to 300 knots.

Al maintained our lock on the number two MIG. I went into burner, closed to within about 4,000 feet range and, with about 20 degrees angle off, fired a Sparrow. It worked perfectly, and I was entranced watching its performance as it tracked right to the MIG, making slight corrections. It exploded right next to the MIG, and I saw pieces of his airplane come off as he instantly pitched up, then down, with vapor streaming behind. This all happened within the space of a few seconds, and I looked left just in time to see the MIG leader right at nine o'clock and pulling hard to get lead on me to start firing. I was looking right down his intake from about 3,500 feet away, and I knew it wouldn't be too long before he started pumping cannon shells at Al and me, but because of our high speed, I had some time to work with. The number three MIG was dead ahead of me, and I had learned long ago, that if I couldn't kill a guy outright in a fight, the next best thing was to convince him he was flying against a wild man and scare him into making a mistake. With that in mind, I deliberately held a near collision course for that number three MIG, roaring right across the top of his cockpit, still in full burner, with my belly no more than ten feet above his canopy. In that split-second as we passed over him I was looking right into his face! I could easily see his big eyeballs behind the goggles, his parachute buckles and straps, his hand on the stick, the switches on the consoles ... I was awfully close to his airplane!

Immediately as I passed over number three, I pulled up hard into a tight barrel roll to the left and into the lead MIG who had never quite managed to achieve a firing position. He took a short look at what I was doing, and elected to go after Tom, who had flown directly through their flight before the fight started. Tom had decided to use the only tactic he knew, the famous "F-4 getaway". That is ... he unloaded, (pushed the nose over until he attained a zero "G" loading on the aircraft) went into full burner, and was really accelerating away. He was shortly down to 500 feet altitude and doing 1.2 mach. I knew there was no way the MIG was ever going to catch him, so I went after my number three MIG, who was probably the least experienced pilot in the fight. He had done a quick 180 degree turn after watching his number two get smoked, and our near collision. He was headed directly home to Phuc Yen with the blinders on. I completed my barrel roll and came down after him in burner. He was cold meat on the table ... no way I could have missed getting him ... he didn't even know I was there and probably wasn't looking. Tom picked precisely that time to re-engage. He pulled 6-7 G's doing it and used up a good bit of his plane's energy in the process, which total effect allowed the MIG leader to rapidly close into a firing position. Tom was using the last half of the accepted tactic of employing the Phantom's superior acceleration to achieve separation, then turning to re-engage on an equal basis. Unfortunately, Tom had not gotten the necessary separation before starting back into the fight, and now he was in serious trouble. It was quite obvious to me that we were going to lose an F-4 and its crew if something drastic didn't happen pretty quick to change the inevitable. So, much as I dearly wanted that second kill, and as sure of it as I was, I gritted my teeth, pulled my machine hard around, and headed back toward Tom and the MIG leader.

As the MIG leader saw me do this, he feinted into me with a quick roll, but he didn't put any "G" on it, so didn't appreciably change his flight path, which was still gaining him firing position on Tom. It was merely an effort to throw me off, and gain him some more time. I wasn't buying, and continued on down to press my attack on him. But the MIG wasn't really concerned about me at that time, which showed he was a pretty heads-up driver. He knew that at these low altitudes, in a position where I had to look down on him, I wasn't going to be able to achieve the radar discrimination necessary to employ Sparrows, and my angle off was too great to use the Sidewinders.

The MIG continued after Tom, and he was now firing. Tom's RIO was LTJG Gary Taylor who was a very fine radar operator and crewmember. However, Gary had his own brand of logic process. He sometimes existed in a world all his own. During this timeframe, with his world on the verge of going down in flames, or worse, Gary had reasoned that since all of the action was behind him, there was really no reason to continue running his radar equipment. He had unstrapped, and was kneeling facing aft in his seat, using his hand held .35mm camera to take pictures of this MIG closing in to shoot him down! Several of the pictures he took clearly showed the muzzle flashes from the MIG's 37mm cannon!

I kept hollering for Tom to roll out and go. I knew that the MIG could never catch him if he would do this simple maneuver, but that if he kept turning, the MIG would eventually pull the correct lead and blast him. Tom never did roll out, but when I got down to the MIG's altitude, we started picking up his return on radar, and were just about to paint him well enough for a lock-on when he abruptly decided to break it off. He showed his saavy again by rolling over and diving right down to the deck. I estimate his altitude must have been about 20 feet, and he was heading straight for China. It was impossible to get any radar discrimination with all the ground return, and the heat seekers in the Sidewinders were buzzing merrily from radiation of the hot sunny earth, so there was no hope of discrimination there either. I followed him for a little while, but he was well aware that with no guns in the Phantom, as long as he stayed low, I couldn't do a thing to him.

Tom had rolled out finally, and was streaking for the coast leaving Al and I far behind. He had a 27 mile head start on us as I broke off and also headed out of North Vietnam. We finally joined up with Tom off the coast,

Officers of VF-151, Oct. 1966 aboard USS Constellation. After two cruises without losing an airplane or flight crewman to enemy action, VF-151 on it's next cruise lost ten of the officers in this picture to the enemy. Of the ten, only four emerged from North Vietnamese prisons at war's end.

just a tad north of Cam Pha.

The weather was clear over the water, and it was a truly beautiful day. We headed south at 500 to 1,000 feet altitude, admiring the view and being careful to stay below the effective envelope of the SA-2 unit near Cam Pha. The sea was a brilliant dark blue with numerous small islands set in it like vivid green jewels in the sunshine. Nothing could have been more serene and peaceful. We had only our fuel state to concern us.

Suddenly there was a sharp explosion in my cockpit, and I started to get some smoke! A quick scan of the instruments showed nothing wrong, and after a bit, the smoke cleared up, but both Al and I were pretty concerned at the time. As it turned out, we had been hit by a single .30 caliber rifle slug, which we figured some farmer had fired from one of those small "peaceful" islands. It had buried itself in a bundle of wiring about four inches from my leg, but caused no great damage.

We found an A-3 tanker who had heard all the commotion of the fight over the radio. Figuring we might be able to use some fuel after all that, he came north to meet us half way. The meeting was not a second too soon for Tom, who was down to 600 pounds of fuel (approximately 10 minutes of flying time at very most). I still had about 1,400 pounds, which would have gotten me back to the ship ... just barely.

One of the more significant gains to come out of our F-4 experiences in the war, was the change in fighter pilot's attitudes toward the multi-crewed fighter plane. When I first jumped into the F-4, with more than 3,000 hours of single engine, single cockpit fighter time behind me, I figured I pretty well knew my business. I could handle the airplane, fire my Sidewinders ... I didn't need any help. That guy in the back seat was just so much ballast, and about all he was going to do for me was keep the airplane within the engineered center of gravity limits. Boy, was I ever premature! I was fortunate enough to have been paired up with two truly outstanding RIOs during my two combat cruises. LTJG Al Johnson worked with me all through that first cruise, and LTJG Jon Steele saved my skin more than just a few times on the second cruise. When those two gents got with me in the combat environment of North Vietnam, I found out how wrong I had been in my early pre-judgement of the value of that second flight officer in the cockpit.

We had extremely good radar coverage from the GCI teams aboard Red Crown. This, coupled with the exceptional airborne firecontrol radar in the F-4, really gave us a big advantage over the F-8 for example, and the MIGs, in being able to set up in an initally favorable position to start a fight. It didn't always work out that way because the North Vietnamese were no pushovers in the GCI coverage of their own country and surrounding geography. But, that's what we always tried for. The F-8 had an acceptably good radar too, but one man was really hard pressed to operate the radar up to its full capability, navigate, and maintain a good lookout doctrine in the intense combat environment, all the while, flying his aircraft in his customary superb manner. When he was doing good radar work, the visual integrity had to suffer, and when he maintained a top notch visual scan, the radar work deteriorated. In any case, the load carried by the driver of a single piloted machine under combat conditions is extreme, and being human, there will naturally be times when the total product is simply not as effective as it could be. In the Phantom, the gent driving could always maintain a first rate visual lookout, while the guy in the back seat could stay on the radar and really get peak performance from it. When the RIO didn't need to be on the scope, he provided another valuable set of eyes to check your six o'clock. Additionally, the RIO could double check the navigation, control knob or switch settings, SAM (Surface-to-Air) or AAA fire control warnings, and a hundred other items that when combined with the pilot's efforts, kept the F-4 "human" performance at an overall higher level of efficiency than the single piloted aircraft. Granted, there are some tactical situations that would not require the full capability of the multi-crewed aircraft, and would benefit by the advantages gained from a smaller, less complex, single piloted machine. But in the North Vietnam environment, the Phantom's crew concept certainly proved itself. I would be hard pressed to estimate the number of F-4's which came back to their home base or carrier that might otherwise have been bagged had it not been for the added dimension of the RIO."

After completion of his second cruise in the war zone, this time in Constellation (CVA-64), LCDR Dan Macintyre was reassigned to VF-121. He had flown 238 combat missions; 208 of them over North Vietnam. He took over the Air Combat Maneuvering training sylabus from LCDR Sam Flynn and further refined it. These early awakenings of the Navy to the need for ACM, eventually led to the formation of the Navy Fighter Weapons School, the now famous "Top Gun" program. Today Dan is flying for American Airlines and is presently based in Chicago. He also holds the rank of captain in the U. S. Naval Air Reserve.

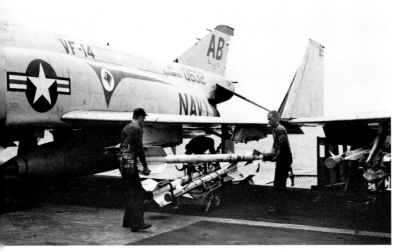

VF-154 F-4B being positioned for launch from Ranger, Gulf of Tonkin, 1968. Flight of three Phantoms is returning from a mission, and about to "break" into the landing pattern. (US Navy)

F-4B approaching America for landing during air-ops cycles off the East Coast, 1966. (US Navy)

Sidewinder loading in the Gulf of Tonkin, aboard FDR, 1966. (US Navy)

KA-3B of VAH-4 refuels F-4B of VF-213 after a strike on North Vietnam in 1968. (US Navy)

F-4B of VF-32 milliseconds prior to launch from JFK. (US Navy)

VF-32 Phantom clearing the angled deck of JFK as it launches from the waist catapult. Later model drooped ailerons and improved boundary layer bleed air (which necessitated "fixing" inboard leading edge slats) have been retrofitted to B models. (US Navy)

Saratoga based F-4B from VF-11"Red Rippers". Navy Phantoms did not often have to fly great distances to target, and often had out-board wing pylons modified to carry ordnance only, as in this case. (370 gallon wing tanks could not be attached) (US Navy)

VF-31 F-4J in 1968 squadron markings. (US Navy)

Phantoms of VF-32 aboard JFK during air ops in the Carribbean, 1968. (US Navy)

VF-14 Phantom is positioned prior to air ops from JFK in the Med, 1969. Plane guard destroyer USS William R. Rush (DD714) is to port. (US Navy)

Nose Development

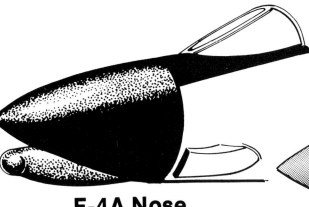

F-4A Nose

F-4B Nose

F-4J Nose

Number one catapult has just fired, and this Swordsman Phantom is seconds from flight off the deck of JFK. Note stabilator in full deflected (nose up) position. (US Navy)

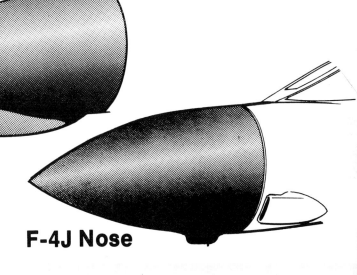

Replenishing a Phantom's oxygen supply, aboard Enterprise. (US Navy)

Phantom of VF-32 aboard JFK during air ops in the Carribbean, 1968. (US Navy)

(Above) F-4J of VF-154 over the Sea of Japan. Tail stripes are Blue, Red, Blue. (US Navy)

(Below) Airborne from the waist cat. Deflected position of ailerons is most evident in this photo. (US Navy)

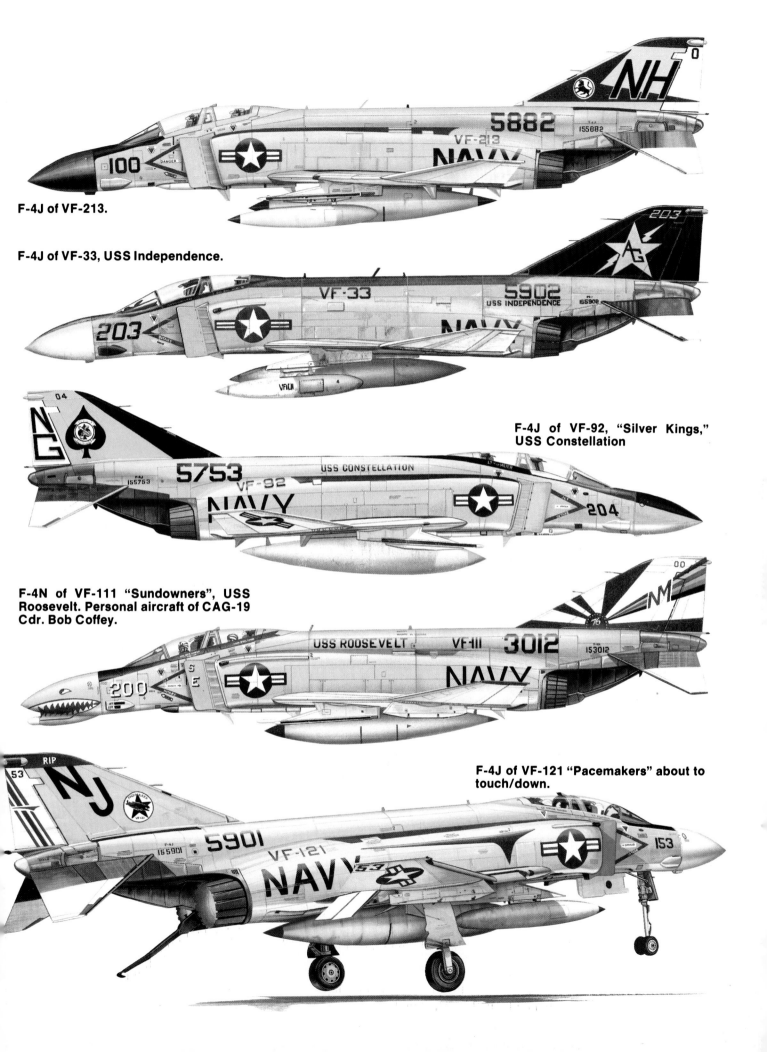

F-4J of VF-213.

F-4J of VF-33, USS Independence.

F-4J of VF-92, "Silver Kings," USS Constellation

F-4N of VF-111 "Sundowners", USS Roosevelt. Personal aircraft of CAG-19 Cdr. Bob Coffey.

F-4J of VF-121 "Pacemakers" about to touch/down.

Refuelling Probe

ECM Antennae

F-4J

F-4N

(Above) Flight deck director positions a Phantom for launch from the Midway, as he braces himself against better than 30 knots of wind at his back. (US Navy)

VF-51 Phantoms sported a version of their namesake (Screaming Eagles) in the early 70's. They referred to it as a supersonic eagle. Others dubbed it "supersonic can-opener". They have since modified their markings. (Harry Walker)

Instantaneous speed acheived in launch is evident in this shot as Phantom has traveled less than 50 feet on catapult, and still could not be "stopped" by the camera. (US Navy)

At the height of Linebacker I, redshirts aboard the Constellation load a TER with Mk 82 bombs on a VF-92 Phantom. (US Navy)

Catapult crewmen attaching the cat bridle to VF-96 Phantom prior to combat mission from the Connie in 1972. This aircraft was assigned to the Navy's aces, Cunningham and Driscoll, though they did not use it to achieve any of their kills. (US Navy)

VF-92 Phantom makes a text-book landing aboard Constellation, touching down between second and third cable, catching third cable with his hook. (US Navy)

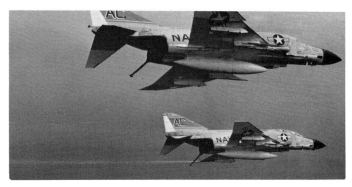

VF-31 Phantoms dump fuel to get down to landing weight as they approach Saratoga's landing pattern. (US Navy)

(Above) F-4J of VF-114 in Bicentennial livery. VF-114 has since traded in their Phantoms for F-14 Tomcats. (Scott Brown)

(Below) Late VF-51 markings consist of black tail, with red stripes. Note intake screens installed as a safety precaution for ground run-up of engines. (FOD ... foreign object damage ... is one of the more costly and preventable maintenance headaches for all jet aircraft). (Scott Brown)

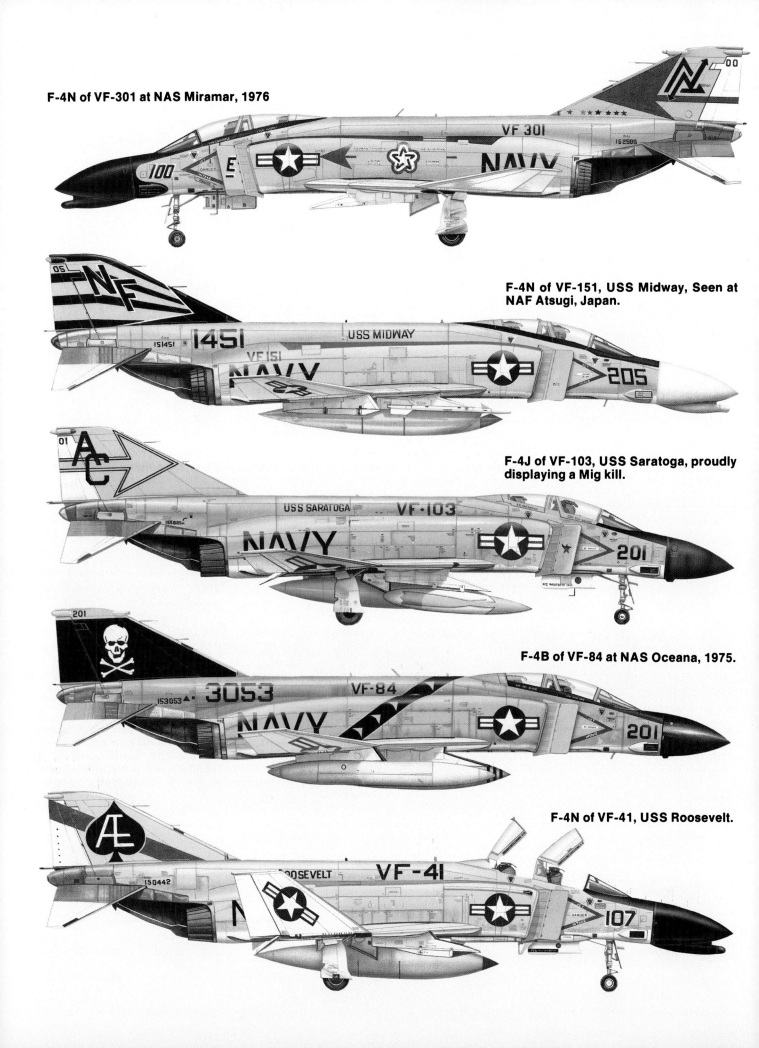

F-4N of VF-301 at NAS Miramar, 1976

F-4N of VF-151, USS Midway, Seen at NAF Atsugi, Japan.

F-4J of VF-103, USS Saratoga, proudly displaying a Mig kill.

F-4B of VF-84 at NAS Oceana, 1975.

F-4N of VF-41, USS Roosevelt.

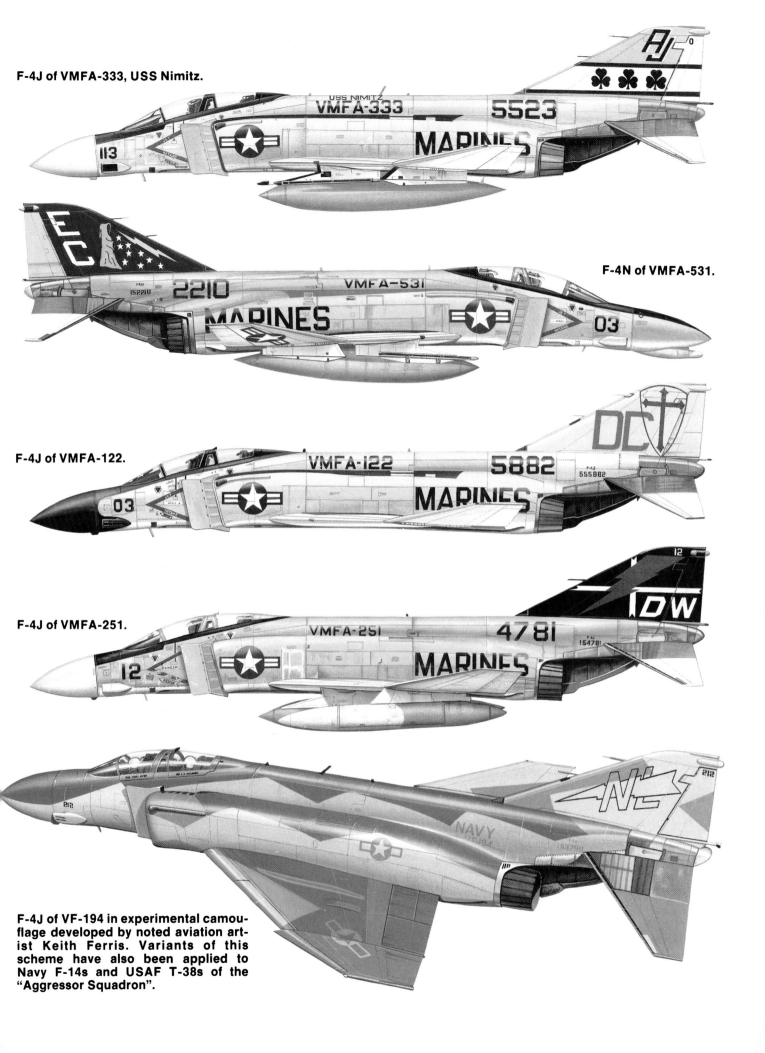

F-4J of VMFA-333, USS Nimitz.

F-4N of VMFA-531.

F-4J of VMFA-122.

F-4J of VMFA-251.

F-4J of VF-194 in experimental camouflage developed by noted aviation artist Keith Ferris. Variants of this scheme have also been applied to Navy F-14s and USAF T-38s of the "Aggressor Squadron".

(Above) Phantom recovers aboard JFK, while Flight Deck Director waits to park it after it clears the arresting gear. (US Navy)

(Below) F-4B's and J of VX-4. Squadron markings consist of medium blue band, outlined in red, with white stars. VX-4 is Navy Air Development Squadron based at Point Mugu, California. (US Navy)

Gloss black F-4J of VX-4, carries white markings. (US Navy)

(Below) Overall gloss red/orange finish of this QF-4B Drone inspired name "Great Pumpkin", which appears on nose. Several older F-4B's have been modified by the Navy for use as target or research drones. This one is assigned to the Naval Air Development Center. (D.W. Fisher via Jim Sullivan)

Ex-Blue Angels F-4J operated by NATC retains overall gloss blue finish, with yellow markings. Blue Angels traded their Phantoms for Skyhawks in an economy move after the energy crisis of 1973. (Peter Mancus via Jim Sullivan)

Marine Phantoms

"Exterminator" and "Chevas Regal", a pair of Marine F-4B's enroute to target in 1971. Though they often carried air-to-air ordnance (as in this instance) Marine Phantoms were almost exclusively employed in ground support role. Only Marine pilots to score Mig kills were on exchange duty with the Air Force when they scored. (USMC)

VMFA-323 F-4B at MCAS Iwakuni. "Blade" ... an F-4B of VMFA-314 enroute to target. RF-4B of VMCJ-1 at NAS Iwakuni in 1971. Marines took delivery of their first Phantoms in 1962, and have set such milestones as 10,000 accident-free hours, (VMFA-251) and 888 hours in 17 days. (VMFA-531) (USMC)

Bicentennial Phantoms

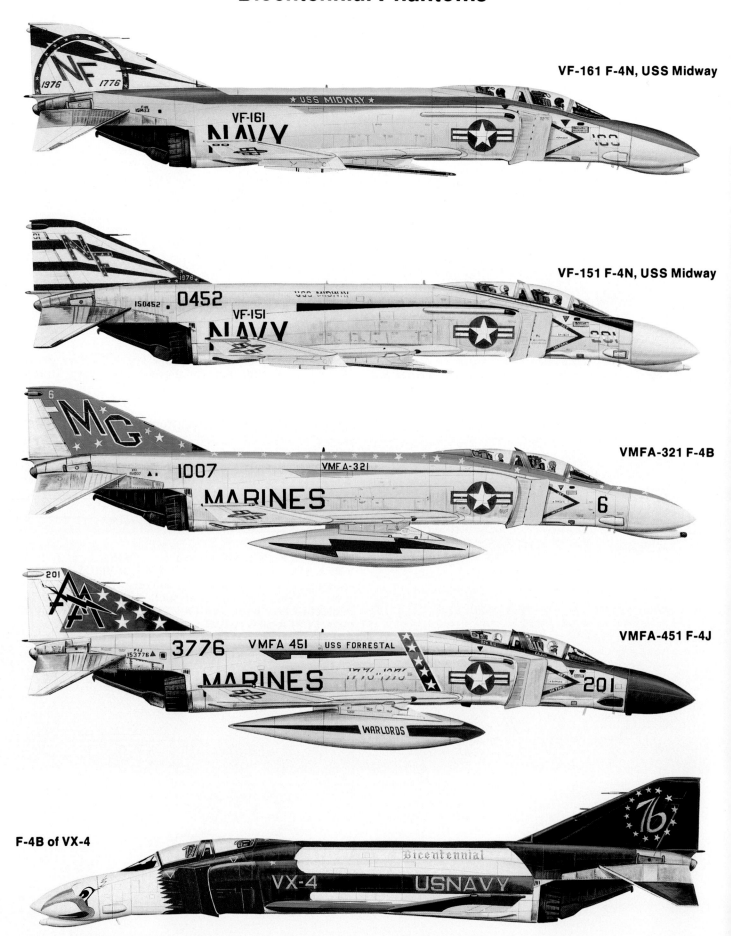

VF-161 F-4N, USS Midway

VF-151 F-4N, USS Midway

VMFA-321 F-4B

VMFA-451 F-4J

F-4B of VX-4

Bicentennial Phantoms

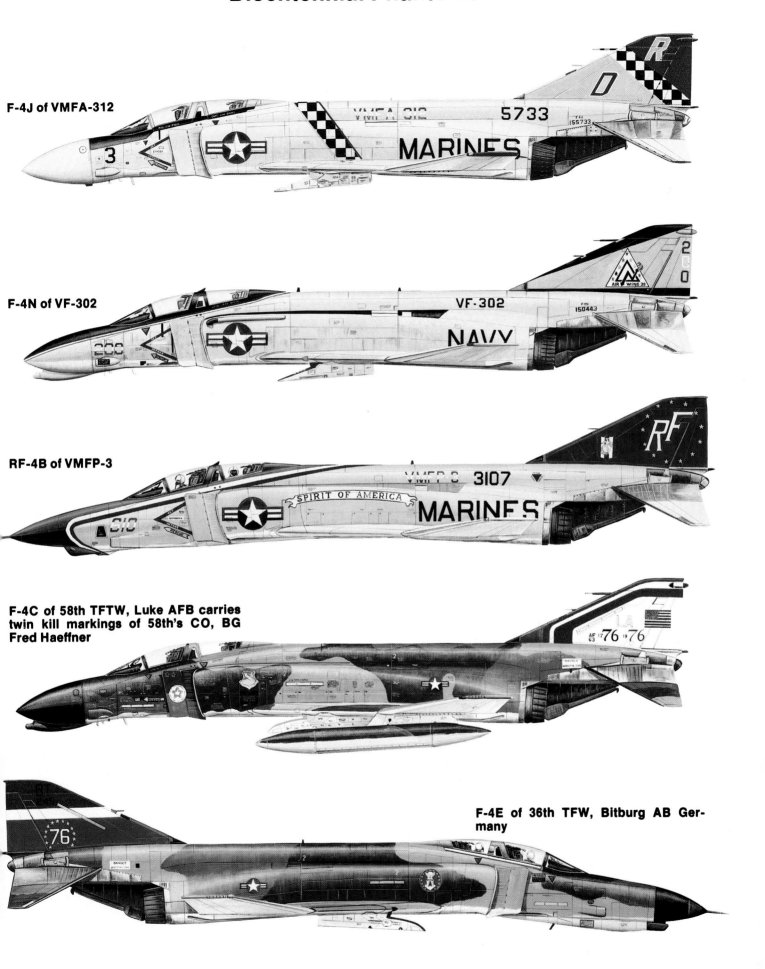

F-4J of VMFA-312

F-4N of VF-302

RF-4B of VMFP-3

F-4C of 58th TFTW, Luke AFB carries twin kill markings of 58th's CO, BG Fred Haeffner

F-4E of 36th TFW, Bitburg AB Germany

VMFA-312 F-4B attached to APU, and ready for quick reaction start. (note pilot's harness hung on boarding ladder.)

VMFA-251 markings. Early markings consisted of black-outlined orange lightning bolt on tail, with squadron badge on fuselage side. (USMC)

VMCJ-2 RF-4B landing at MCAS Cherry Point, North Carolina in 1973. (Jim Sullivan)

VMFA-115 F-4B at NAS Naha, Okinawa, January, 1968, is a well-worn combat veteran.

(Above) Marine Phantom approaching the cross wind runway at Chu Lai with hook down. Field arresting gear will stop the F-4 in 600 feet. (Below) VMFA-323 F-4B catches the field arresting gear at Danang, in the first test of the gear. Danang was a primary divert field for all aircraft flying combat missions over North Vietnam, and the arresting gear was necessary to ensure safe landings by combat-damaged aircraft. It went into operation in 1966. (USMC)

(Above) VMFA-232 F-4J, with drag chute out, lands at Cubi Point in the Phillipines, August, 1974. (USMC) (Above Right) "Clean" F-4J of VMFAT-201 at NAF Washington, D.C., 1974. (Dr. J. G. Handelman) (Right) F-4B of VMFA-122 at NAS North Island in 1975 appears to have nose radome borrowed from VF-III Phantom. (Peter Mancus via Jim Sullivan)

(Above) VMFA-235 F-4J carries red nose and tail band, white star-spangled, and Death Angel on rudder. MCAS Kaneohe Bay, Hawaii, 1975. (Dr. J.G. Handelman)

(Below) Note Pineapple on splitter plate of MCAS Kaneohe Bay based F-4J of VMFA-212. (Dr. J.G. Handelman)

YRF-4C 62-12200 in it's latest configuration, with fly by wire control system and canards.

F-4B of VF-51 in latest markings carried by "Screaming Eagles".

F-4J of VF-74 at full power on the catapult of USS Nimitz, seconds prior to
launch

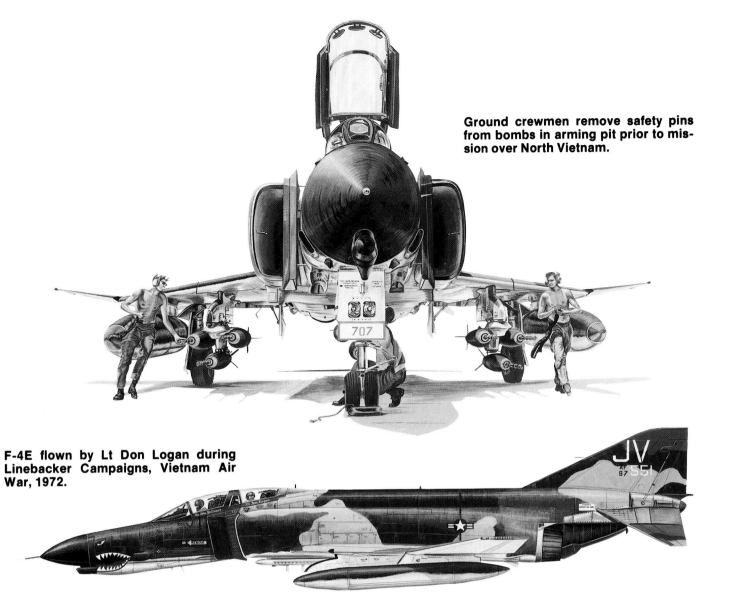

Ground crewmen remove safety pins from bombs in arming pit prior to mission over North Vietnam.

F-4E flown by Lt Don Logan during Linebacker Campaigns, Vietnam Air War, 1972.

Main instrument panels of an F-4E. (Left) Pilot's panel. (Below) Radar Operator's panel. (McDonnel Douglas)

USAF Phantoms

(Above) One of two Navy F-4B's which were loaned to the Air Force for testing and evaluation arrives at TAC Headquarters, Langley AFB, Virginia, in January of 1962. Original Air Force designation for the F-4 was F-110A. (USAF)

(Below) The first production F-4C at Edwards AFB in 1964. It is shown loaded with LAU-10/Mk 24 flare pilot pods on multiple ejector racks. Early Air Force Phantoms carried same color scheme as Navy F-4's. (USAF)

Fourth F-4C at Edwards in 1964 tested 750 pound bombs on TER's (wing hardpoints) and MER (centerline). (USAF)

Rear cockpit, F-4C. (McDonnell Douglas)

First production RF-4C at Edwards AFB for testing, 1965. Note that it carries the large test nose boom, which is instrumented for precise yaw, roll, and pitch readings. (USAF)

F-4C-18-MC of the 15th TFW landing at George AFB, California in 1963. (Jerry Geer)

F-4C's enroute to targets over the north early in the war. They are loaded with 750 lb. bombs, which was one of the favorite weapons for use against the North's industry. (USAF)

Crew Chief of RF-4C about to send his charge off on a mission over North Vietnam in the early sixties. Reconnaissance aircraft were among the first to fly combat missions over the North. (USAF)

Latest version of USAF F-4E has been retrofitted with slats and TISEO on port leading edge of wing.

Phantom FGR-2 of No. 41 Sqd. RAF.

FGR-2 of III Squadron, RAF

F-4F of 71st Fighter Interceptor Wing, West German Air Force, based at Wittmund AFB with experimental camouflage, August 1976.

Early model F-4D of the 8th TFW enroute to target in 1966. Despite official protestations that there was no "bomb shortage", this photo is graphic evidence that missions were flown with less than the optimum bomb load, in an effort to build up the numbers of sorties flown. Tail stripes are blue and yellow. Note Phantom riding an eight ball on the rudder. (USAF)

F-4C's are lined up on the ramp at Cam Ranh Bay AB, Vietnam, December 1970. Waiting for the signal to roll. (USAF)

F-4D of the 389th TFS, 12th TFW at Phu Cat AB, Vietnam, 1970. It is loaded with 500 and 1,000 pound bombs, with fuse extenders. (Norman E. Taylor)

First F-4E's to arrive in Southeast Asia taxi in at Korat AB, Thailand in November, 1968. They are shown in standard long-range ferry configuration of two 370 gallon wing tanks, and centerline 600 gallon tank. Pod on inboard wing station was often used to carry crew luggage. (USAF)

F-4E on the flightline at Takhli AB, Thailand in April, 1969. It is equipped with inboard TER's and outboard MER's. Starboard TER carries an ECM pod. (USAF)

Loran equipped F-4D of the 25th TFS, 8th TFW, which was based at Ubon AB Thailand, during a September, 1970 visit to Phu Cat AB, South Vietnam. (Norman E. Taylor)

F-4D's of 8th TFW prepare for a mission from Ubon in 1970. They are armed with 500 lb. bombs, with fuse extenders. (USAF)

F-4D Chaff Bomber of the 8th TFW over Vietnam, 1968, (Major Al Piccirillo via Norman E. Taylor)

8th TFW F-4D returning to Thailand after a strike on North Vietnam during Linebacker Campaign of 1972. (Don Logan)

F-4D Radar

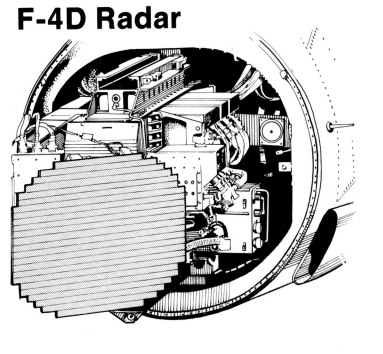

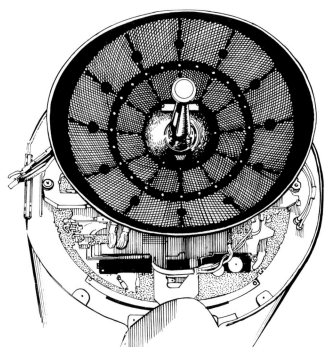

F-4E Radar

8th TFW Phantoms approach KC-135 tanker over Vietnam. (USAF)

(Right) Mig Killer Lt. William Hargrove checks preflight forms prior to September, 1972 mission from Udorn AB, Thailand. F-4 is loaded in air-to-air configuration, with Sidewinders and ECM pod on inboard wing stations. Terry cloth towels replaced silk scarves among the pilots of the 432nd TRW during the heat of this aerial campaign. (USAF)

F-4D Laser Bomber carries 1000 lb. Laser guided bombs on port outboard and starboard inboard wing stations, Pave Knife Laser designator pod on port inboard, and 370 gallon wing tank on starboard outboard stations. (USAF)

F-4E Laser bomber gets final check in arming pit prior to May, 1972 mission. ECM pods are carried in forward Sparrow missile wells. (USAF)

ECM Pods

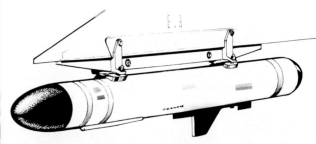

Westinghouse ALQ-101 combination noise and deception jamming pod

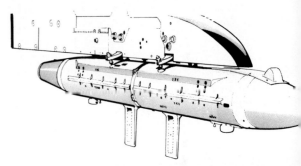

General Electric ALQ-87 barrage noise jammer pod

Logan's Story

Captain Don Logan holds the unlucky distinction of having been on the wrong end of an F-4 Mig kill, but was fortunate enough to have survived to tell of his experiences.

He enlisted in the Air Force in August, 1969, went through OTS and NAV School, and was assigned to George AFB for F-4 training. Upon graduation from the F-4 RTU, he was assigned to the 469th TFS, 388th TFW, flying missions out of Korat RTAB. Prior to being shot down, he participated in the Linebacker bombing campaign over North Vietnam. In addition to his career as an Air Force Officer and Aircrewman, he is a student of aviation history, and as such, his assessment of the Phantom is particularly important.

"In my opinion, the F-4 is a great "do everything" aircraft. It could do just about everything well, but was not the best at any one given thing. The F-106 is a better interceptor, for instance, and the F-111 is a much better strike bomber. I think the F-4 will be around for a long time to come, and will go down in history, along with the P-51 and Bf-109 as the best fighter of it's time. From the point of view of a NAV doing the job of WSO, the best place to be is in the right seat of the F-111 ... not the back of an F-4. The WSO in the 111 controls the mission of the aircraft, namely Radar Bombing at night or in bad weather. The F-111 can do this better than any other airplane presently in existance. Unless he was running a radar intercept, or operating the Loran or Laser designator, the WSO in an F-4 had little to do other than act as a second set of eyes to keep his pilot out of trouble. As the F-4 is updated with the new systems like TISEO and Loran, the WSO will become more important ... and much busier.

Two of the combat missions that really stand out in my mind were completely different, and point up the diverse roles the Phantom operated in during the Vietnam War. During June of 1972 we were tasked to interdict the supply routes in North Vietnam, specifically the Northeast and Northwest railroads which ran from the Hanoi area to the Communist Chinese border. One such mission had us fragged against a stretch of the Northeast Railroad. The area we were concentrating on was a rail yard in a river valley located between two ridge lines. The rail yard had quite a few pieces of rolling stock, and since the F-4's were carrying twelve Mk. 82 five hundred pound bombs each, a tactic of four passes of three bombs each was decided on. We flew the classic wheel pattern overhead, while the aircraft would drop out of the wheel one at a time to make their run. The bomb run took us below the ridgelines on either side of the railroad. We had to jink constantly going down final to negate the tracking of the AAA, which was crossfiring at us from the tops of the ridgelines. We got outstanding results on this mission, destroying several pieces of rolling stock and hundreds of feet of railroad track. We got one secondary explosion from a string of tank cars that caused a fireball 750 feet in diameter. All aircraft returned from this mission without sustaining even minor damage.

My last mission took place on July 5, 1972. I had had July 4 off and was not scheduled to fly on the 5th either, but one of the other Weapon Systems Officers in my flight got sick, and I was asked to replace him. My pilot was also my flight commander, and we had flown together before.

Our shark-nosed F-4E was number four in a flight of four escorts for twelve F-4E bombers, which were fragged on a target close to Kep airfield, about 30 miles northeast of Hanoi. As escort, it was our job to stick close to the bombers, and to engage any Migs that came up to chal-

Lt. Ron Henning in the cockpit of his F-4E during 1973 "peacekeeping" deployment to Thailand.

lenge them. As escort, we stayed on the strike flight's frequency, and did not receive any direct broadcast Mig information from Red Crown (the Navy Cruiser that orbited off the coast of North Vietnam supplying MIGCAP flights with radar location of enemy fighters) or from the Air Force EC-121. (which supplied similar information from it's orbit over Laos.)

The strike flights ingressed to the target with no problem, and as they made their dive bomb passes on the target, we continued past them and began a 180 degree turn, so that we could pick them up as they came off the target. As we were in the turn, I saw the number two airplane in our flight get hit by a missile which seemed to come from below the flight. The F-4 immediately burst into flames, and I saw the two crewmembers eject. We had completed the turn, and had just rolled out when we got a radio call from the backseater of the lead aircraft telling us to break hard right. As we rolled, I felt a violent jar, and looked out to see the outboard portion of the left wing, past the wing fold, badly damaged. I then scanned the cockpit instruments and noted that the left engine tachometer was reading zero, and the right tach was winding down past 30% RPM. I asked the A/C if he still had control of the airplane. He replied that he did, and I told him to turn to three o'clock, which was the closest distance "feet wet". If we could make the Gulf of Tonkin, we were pretty well assured of getting picked up by the Navy after we ejected. I told him that the engine circuit breakers on my right circuit breaker panel were popped, but I was holding them in, and for him to try an airstart on the right engine, which was still windmilling. While he attempted the airstart, I looked over my right shoulder ... and there was a North Vietnamese Mig-21 flying close formation on us! As soon as he saw me looking at him, he rolled over us and split S down behind us, into a cloud deck, getting away from the rest of our flight. Both of his missile rails were empty. I later found out that he was one of a flight of two Mig-21's that shot both of us down.

We had been hit at about 20,000 feet, and as we passed 10,000 feet, it became clear that an airstart was not going to happen, and that we were going to have to jump out. The A/C asked me if I was ready to eject, and I told him yes ... command eject both of us. I heard him count down 3, 2, 1, and as he said "one" I saw the canopy leave the airplane and felt the boom before I could do anything else ... and there I was ... hanging in my chute 5,000 feet over North Vietnam. I checked my canopy, made the four line modification that would allow me to steer the parachute, and deployed my survival kit and raft on the lowering line, so that it wouldn't be attached directly to the harness under my seat when I landed. (Lot's of people have been injured in landings with all that gear in the wrong place.) I got on my survival radio and made a call, giving my callsign, and stating that both the A/C and I were out of the airplane with good chutes. Worse luck ... we were going down in a populated area. I could see the people in the fields below looking up and pointing at me. I saw about two acres of trees a little ways away, and steered towards it, hoping to find a place to hide. I made the trees alright ... but I had too much forward speed and broke a rib or two, as well as cutting myself up pretty badly ... all this on top of the dislocated shoulder I had suffered in the ejection into the 450 knot airstream past our airplane. Still and all, I was on the ground safely, and was able to move. I released my chute, grabbed a few essentials from the survival kit, and moved out. Within ten minutes I ran into some real thick underbrush, and decided to hide out until night.

Within ten minutes I heard shots, dogs barking, and voices shouting in Vietnamese. In another twenty minutes a group of about a dozen farmers, armed with everything from Ak-47's to flintlock muskets, found me and marched me out to a road, where they handed me over to the North Vietnamese Army. I was put on a truck and taken to the Hanoi Hilton, where I remained until March 29, 1973. I left Hanoi on the last airplane to take POW's out of North Vietnam, 267 days after being shot down.

RF-4 Nose

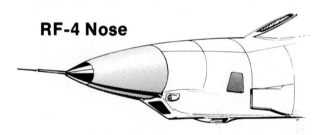

Photoflash Cartridge Ejector

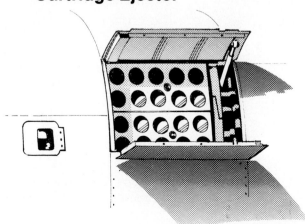

RF-4C of the 33rd TRTS, 363rd TRW, Shaw AFB, SC. at Kelly AFB, Texas, February, 1973. (Norman E. Taylor)

RF-4C of the Alabama ANG.

KC-97L of the Missouri ANG refuels Ramstein-based F-4E's in the skies over Europe. (USAF)

Slatted F-4E of USAFE takes on fuel from KC-97L of Illinois ANG over Germany, June, 1976. It carries practice Sidewinder Missile. (Lou Drendel)

Shark-mouthed RF-4C of 26th TRW at Ramstein AB, Germany. (Michel C. Klaver)

F-4E of the 32nd TFS taxies at Soesterberg, Netherlands with aerial target. (Michel C. Klaver)

RF-4C of the 17th TRS at Zweibrucken, West Germany, positioned for engine run-up tests, with hold-back cable attached to arresting hook. Note engine access panels open for maintenance. (Michel C. Klaver)

RF-4C of the 17th TRS, 26th TFW, based at Zweibrücken, was photographed at Baden Söllingen, West Germany during May, 1975 Royal Flush NATO Exercise. Red-/Black/White tail markings were applied for the occasion. (AAPP)

Nose Development

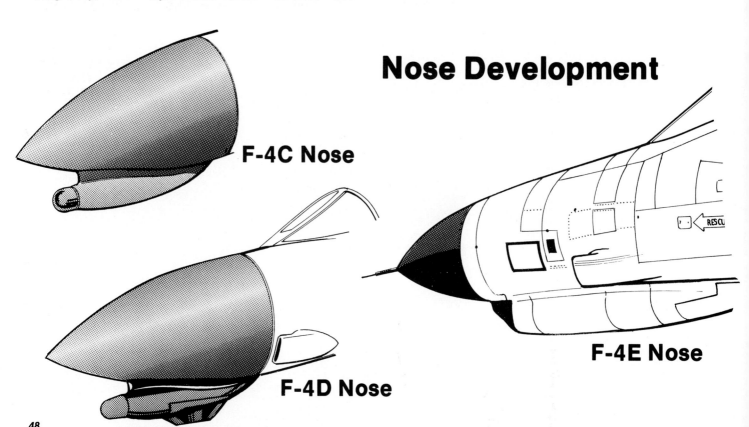

F-4C Nose

F-4D Nose

F-4E Nose

Slats Story

Though the Phantom was never intended as an air-superiority fighter, events in the Vietnam Air War forced it into this role. When it became apparent that the F-4's continued combat life might depend upon improvements in it's air combat manuevering capabilities, the engineers at McDonnell Aircraft Company got busy.

The installation of leading edge slats was the culmination of a program of combat agility improvement conducted by NASA and MCAIR beginning in 1970. The test-bed aircraft for the slats program was the workhorse 62-12200, the original YRF-4B. It was evaluated by the USAF, USN, Israeli Air Force, and MCAIR Flight Test, in a program designated "Project Agile Eagle". Ironically, much of the operational testing was done by the Israeli Air Force under actual combat conditions, in an effort to divert attention from the improved F-4. It was felt that less-than-knowledgeable congressional critics of the F-15 Eagle might seize upon the improved F-4 as an excuse to delay or deny full F-15 funding. While the leading edge slats do improve F-4 performance dramatically, they do not make it a match for the F-15, anymore than the proverbial sow's ear can be turned into a silk purse.

MCAIR engineers, in their effort to improve the F-4's energy maneuverability, looked at several alternative methods of providing the best blend of higher usable CL at reduced drag, improved handling characteristics at high angles-of-attack, suitability for takeoff/landing high-lift configurations, and compatibility with F-4 wing planform and structural concept. Candidates for implementing these improvements included leading edge flaps and slats, leading edge camber, trailing edge flaps, and various combinations of these. Wind tunnel tests showed significant improvements in energy maneuverability with slats as well as with leading edge flaps. But at high angles of attack, the slat equipped wing showed considerably better lift and drag characteristics than the wing with leading edge flaps. Tests with Fowler flaps and leading edge camber also showed the superiority of the slat equipped wing. The slatted wing was settled on, and fixed slats were installed on 62-12200. The flight tests demonstrated performance in excess of that indicated by the wind tunnel tests. A bonus of the slat equipped wing was an increase in lateral directional stability at high angles of attack.

Addition of leading edge two-position slats to the airplane is accomplished within the existing capabilities of the utility hydraulic, pneumatic and electrical systems. The changes have a minimal effect on the basic structure, and are as follows:
*Installation of an inboard maneuvering slat and actuating mechanism
*Installation of an outer maneuvering slat and actuating mechanism
*Outer and inner wing strengthening to allow retention of the load factor capabilities and to provide satisfactory fatigue life.
*Deletion of leading and trailing edge boundary layer control.

The Navy, long a proponent of air combat maneuvering with the F-4, and with no new air superiority fighter of it's own on the horizon, would love to have had the slat-equipped Phantom, but this last modification killed a Navy slatted F-4, at least for the time being. (BLC is an operational necessity for Navy Phantoms, to allow slower carrier approach speeds.) Work has continued on a slatted Phantom for the Navy though, and indications are that it may soon be a reality, with the Navy designation F-4S.

How Slats Work

The leading edge slats are operable in order to retain the high speed performance. The slats automatically extend as the airplane angle of attack reaches 11.5 units on the cockpit indicator and retract when 10.5 units is indicated. The essential element in determining the point at which the slats would be deployed is the point at which the slatted wing drag becomes less than the unslatted wing. Ideally, extension and retraction would occur at the same point and would vary with Mach number as the drag crossover point varied. In practice, however, extension and retraction cannot occur at the same point since slat oscillation will occur if flying at this angle of attack. To avoid this, the slat retraction angle of attack has been established at an angle of attack one unit less than the extension angle of attack. These slat actuation points are within the AOA range where the drag and pitching moment characteristics, slats extended or retracted, are nearly equal; as a result slat actuation transients are negligible. Slat extension is limited to the speed range below 600 knots calibrated air speed by an airspeed sensitive override switch.

TISEO
(Target Identification System Electro-Optical)

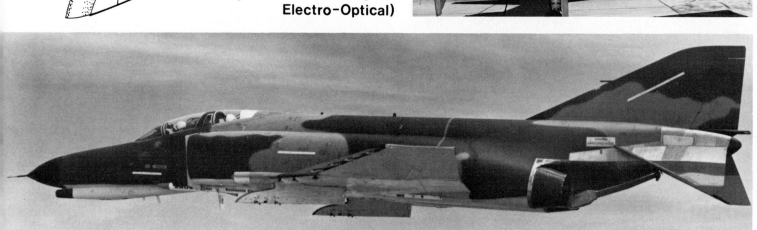

(Above) Latest version of the F-4E for USAF has slatted wing and TISEO installed on port inboard leading edge of wing. (McDonnell Douglas)

(Below) Navy tested leading edge slats on this F-4J. (McDonnell Douglas)

Wild Weasel Phantoms. F-4E (Above) and F-4C (Below) have been modified with extensive ECM and SAM sup-pression equipment to perform in the Wild Weasel role. (McDonnell Douglas)

Leading Edge Flap

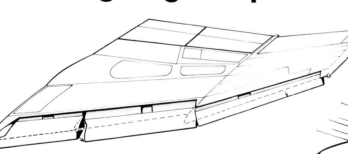

Leading Edge Slat

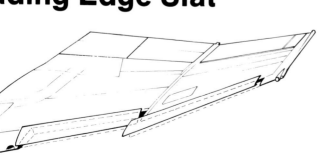

Slat Activating Mechanism

The Saga of 62-12200

Scheduled to roll off the production line as a Navy F-4B, 12200 instead became the prototype RF-4, serving as the testbed for future reconnaissance Phantoms. It remained at McDonnell Aircraft to become the prototype for the F-4E and F-4F, with the installation of the first nose-mounted Vulcan cannon. It was returned to RF configuration for it's role in "Project Agile Eagle", testing the first leading edge slats for the Phantom. It was also fitted with a Beryllium rudder for concurrent advanced materials research. Still at MACAIR, it received a new paint scheme for the most ambitious Phantom modifications to date, as it was fitted with a fly-by-wire control system which will be the standard of fighters for the future. It was later fitted with canards for more testing of advanced control systems. It is flying proof of the versatility and adaptability of the basic Phantom design.

Export Phantoms

The career of the Phantom is inextricably bound to international politics, and it was a unique combination of British politics and McDonnell farsightedness that resulted in the Phantom's becoming an international fighter.

As far back as 1962, McDonnell engineers had considered the installation of the Rolls Royce Spey engines in the Phantom. The RB-168 would offer increased thrust, lower fuel consumption and up to a 30 percent increase in range. Probably for United States political reasons, the Spey was not ordered for American versions of the Phantom, but the fact that it could be adapted to the basic airframe prompted the British to look at the Phantom with increasing interest as their defense budgets climbed during the development of the Hawker P1154 VTOL Strike Fighter. The P1154 fell victim to the malaise of the day ... commonality ... as the British government stuck to their insistance that both RAF and Royal Navy versions be identical. The Phantom was waiting in the wings, and in 1964 Britain became the first foreign government to buy the Phantom. It was an auspicious event in the Phantom's history, for it paved the way for eventual sales to eight other countries.

Phantom FGR-2 of RAF Squadron 17, based at Bruggen, West Germany.

FGR-2 of 31 Squadron, RAF, Bruggen.

FGR-2 of 6 Squadron, Coningsby, UK, in 1968 markings. (All photos by Michel C. Klaver)

FGR-2 of RAF Squadron 41, carries centerline reconnaissance pod and latest squadron markings. (see color
side view for earlier markings) (Michel C. Klaver)

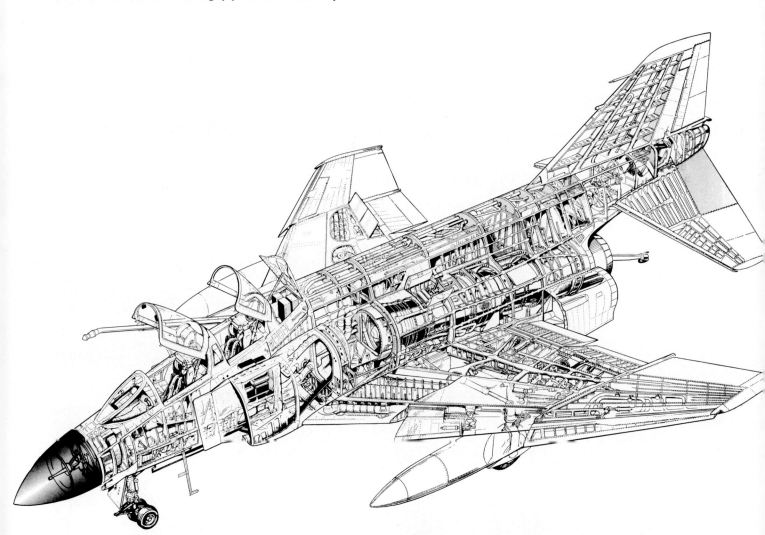

F-4K/M

F-4K of 892 Squadron, Royal Navy during 1971 visit to USS Independence from British carrier Ark Royal. (US Navy)

892 Squadron F-4K during 1975 visit to NAS Oceana. ECM equipment is carried atop vertical fin. (Jim Sullivan)

FG-1 of 767 Squadron, Royal Navy, at Yeovilton, UK. 767 Squadron was disbanded in 1972. (Michel C. Klaver)

FGR-2 of No. 2 Squadron, RAF. (Michel C. Klaver)

F-4K/M Exhaust

F-4B Exhaust

F-4J Exhaust

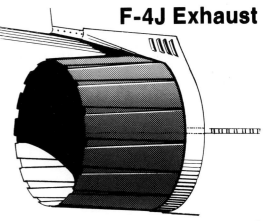

(Left) FGR-2 of No. 2 Squadron, RAF, equipped with strike camera pod. (under intake) (Gunter Grondstein)

FGR-2's of 31 Squadron, RAF, Bruggen, West Germany. In photos below, dark circle on nose gear door is radar altimeter antenna common to all Phantom variants. The Phantoms are carrying practice Sparrow missile and centerline Vulcan gun pod. In photo at bottom, note that auxiliary air door in fuselage side is in full open position. Squadron insignia is green and yellow checkerboard, with yellow star, green wreath, red bow, on a white background. RAF Phantoms based in Germany have duplicated much of stencilling in both English and German. (Michel C. Klaver)

(Above) RF-4E of West German Luftwaffe Squadron AG-52 as it appeared at NATO Exercise Royal Flush XVIII, Bremgarten April, 1975. (Gunter Grondstein)

RF-4E's of West German Luftwaffe AG-51 (Right) and AG-52 (Below) Political reasons for German acquisition of the Phantom are U.S. insistence that Germany pay for part of the cost of maintaining U.S. personnel in Germany. (Michel C. Klaver)

(Above Left & Right) F-4F of JG-74 carrying aerial tow target. Bundesluftwaffe made decision to purchase the F-4F in 1971. 175 are to be delivered. (Bundesluftwaffe)

Federal Republic of Germany builds many of the components for the F-4F, and for American F-4E's. Standard West German camouflage of grey and dark green is applied to majority of their Phantoms.

(Above & Left) Exception to the camouflage rule is this JG-74 F-4F, which sports experimental scheme in three shades of Blue-Grey. (see color illustration on rear cover.)

JG-74 flightline, 1976.

(Above) F-4F taking off from Lambert Field during McDonnell tests. F-4F was the first Phantom variant to introduce the slatted wing operationally. (McDonnell Douglas)

(Below & Bottom) Australia flew F-4E's on loan from USAF, while awaiting delivery of their F-111's. Their F-4's have since been returned to the U.S. They were finished in standard USAF camouflage patterns. (Michel C. Klaver and McDonnell Douglas)

Ageing USAF F-4C's were delivered to the Spanish Air Force in 1971. They were refurbished by CASA and delivered to 121 and 122 Squadrons of the 12th Wing, at Torrejon AB. They are finished in standard USAF camouflage patterns. 122 Squadron Phantoms carry the famous cat insignia on their tails. (AAPP photo Above, Michel C. Klaver Left & Below)

Japanese F-4EJ's are equipped for defensive (air superiority) duties only. Three Japanese fighter-interceptor squadrons are equipped with 80 F-4EJ aircraft, which are license built in Japan. Japan also operates one squadron of RF-4E's. (McDonnell Douglas & Michel C. Klaver.)

Turkey operates two squadrons of F-4E's, a total of 40 aircraft. They are finished in standard USAF camouflage, and are the latest "International" version of the Phantom. (McDonnell Douglas)

SUU-16/A Gun Pod

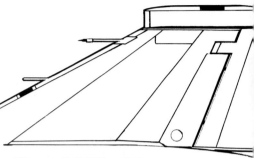

(Left) International F-4E with U.S. insignia, in Israeli camouflage.

F-4K Tail

(Below) Israeli F-4E's over Jerusalem. (McDonnell Douglas) Israel has operated the F-4 since 1969, and their Phantoms have seen extensive combat, in both ground attack and air superiority roles. 6 IDF/AF squadrons operate 204 F-4E's, but Israeli security has effectively masked any definitive breakdown of numbers of squadrons, or how many aircraft are assigned to each. (It varies) It is felt certain that the Israeli Air Force contains more than one Phantom ace, but their names and accounts of their exploits will remain secret until Israel's national security is more fully assured.

(Above & Right) Greece operates 2 fighter squadrons with 38 International F-4E's, which are finished in standard USAF camouflage. (McDonnell Douglas)

Not shown is South Korean Phantom. South Korea operates four squadrons of a mixture of F-4D and E's (total of 72 aircraft). They are painted in standard USAF camouflage.

Iran has operated the Phantom since 1968, beginning with the F-4D (Below), and continuing with their acquisition of the latest International version of the F-4E (Right). The Persian Gulf power operates ten fighter-bomber squadrons of F-4's (32 F-4D, 141 F-4E) which have both Sidewinder and Sparrow capability, and Maverick Air-to-surface missile provision. Iranian camouflage is illustrated in color side view on rear cover. (McDonnell Douglas)